How to Overcome the 10-Year Glitch

*By Margot Maurice
and
John Gallagher*

First Edition

cdp
CRYSTAL DREAMS
publishing

Oshawa, Ontario

How to Overcome the 10-Year Glitch
by Margot Maurice and John Gallagher

Managing Editor:	Kevin Aguanno
Acquisitions Editor:	Sarah Schwersenska
Copy Editor:	Susan Andres
Typesetting:	Peggy LeTrent
Cover Design:	Troy O'Brien
eBook Conversion:	Agustina Baid

Published by: Crystal Dreams Publishing
(a division of Multi-Media Publications Inc.)
Box 58043, Rosslynn RPO, Oshawa, Ontario, Canada, L1J 8L6.

http://www.crystaldreamspublishing.com/

All rights reserved. No part of this book may be reproduced or transmitted in any form or by any means, electronic or mechanical, including photocopying, recording or by any information storage and retrieval system, without written permission from the publisher, except for the inclusion of brief quotations in a review.

Copyright © 2009 by Crystal Dreams Publishing

Paperback	ISBN-10: 1-59146-149-9	ISBN-13: 9781591461494
Adobe PDF ebook	ISBN-10: 1-59146-225-8	ISBN-13: 9781591462255
Mobipocket PRC ebook	ISBN-10: 1-59146-226-6	ISBN-13: 9781591462262
Microsoft LIT ebook	ISBN-10: 1-59146-227-4	ISBN-13: 9781591462279
Palm PDB ebook	ISBN-10: 1-59146-228-2	ISBN-13: 9781591462286

Published in Canada. Printed in the United States of America and England.

CIP data available from the publisher.

Table of Contents

Chapter 1
Introducing the 10-Year Glitch 5

Chapter 2
No Better Time to Live 11

Chapter 3
The Risky Business Called Change 21

Chapter 4
Tolerane—The Second Great Virtue 27

Chapter 5
Am I Who I Want to Be? 35

Chapter 6
Feeling at Home With the Family 47

Chapter 7
The Highest Form of Expectation 55

Chapter 8
A Lesson in Learning 63

Chapter 9
It is a Long Road That Has No Signposts 73

Chapter 10
The Elusive Desire Called Freedom 81

Chapter 11
Magic is Not an Illusion 89

Chapter 12
You Are Only as Old as Your Age 95

Chapter 13
Wake up to Your Dream *103*

Chapter 14
What on Earth Are We Doing Here? *111*

Chapter 15
The View is Clear From an Open Mind *117*

Chapter 16
Worthy of Imitation *121*

Chapter 17
A Rare and Precious Gift *127*

Chapter 18
The Space Where Earth and Spirit Meet *133*

Chapter 19
Happy New Beginning *139*

Chapter 20
It is All in the Mind *153*

Chapter 21
The Motivated Mind *163*

Chapter 22
Moods and Emotions *171*

Chapter 23
The Mind and Memory *177*

Chapter 24
Motivation in Action *183*

About the Authors 189

CHAPTER ONE

Introducing The 10-Year Glitch

Up to this point in the history of the universe and applying to every nation on this planet, **recurring incidents** along with **repeating trends and patterns** have played a major role in shaping many aspects of the earthly experience. *"What goes around comes around"* is a pithy explanation of the phenomenon, as is, *"Nothing new under the sun."*

The 10-Year Glitch evolved from the study of the cyclic nature of life and living. The authors identified seven recurring questions of life (detailed in chapter two) that play vital, demanding roles in every person's journey through life, from arrival to departure and all points between. The points between are made up of ten-year spans, and the authors were surprised to find that one or more of the seven recurring questions of life exerts its positive or negative influence during each decade.

Dealing with the questions as they arise is one of the most important elements of living in order to obtain a true quality of life experience. Not knowing about the recurring questions of life, or ignoring their relevance, energy, or constructive/ destructive abilities, is a major contributing reason for too many ups and downs in what should and could be a relatively smooth and enjoyable journey through life.

Dealing with the questions often requires courage, but the reward is the avoidance of mistakes (if there is truly such a thing as a mistake) and poor decisions regarding money, relationships, careers, social choices, personal growth, and spiritual well-being—any and all of which will contribute to the dreaded 10-Year Glitch during one or more of the decades.

Decade One: Pre-teenage Years. Dependence.

The pre-teen years of life are shaped by rules and influences based on dependency; there is a total reliance on others for guidance.

Decade Two: The Teenage Years. Independence.

The rules change dramatically as the former pre-teens now want to break the shackles of dependency and make the rules to suit themselves rather than others. It is a time of inevitable conflict when inexperience challenges experience, and the first recurring question of life exerts its influence as the teenager seeks an identity.

> *Am I who I want to be?* is a recurring question at various times during a life span, but during the teenage years, it could be paraphrased as *"Why won't they let me be who I want to be?"* "They," of course, refers to any authority figure with legitimate power to question the teenagers' ideas and motivations.

Decade Three: The Twenties. Striving (Phase One).

These are the initial ambitious years, the career years, the years of striving for a place in the scheme of things. An abundance of energy fuels burning desires, plans are plentiful, and the body is at its peak—able to satisfy the demands of a restless, yearning mind. A mentality of *"It's all got to happen in the next ten years"* supplies a driving motivation for whatever success is imagined and anticipated. Most of the recurring questions of life will surface during this and the following decade.

Decade Four: The Thirties. Striving (Phase Two)

Am I where I should be? is the recurring question posed early in this decade.

If the answer is a genuine yes, the striving can continue unabated with almost as much zeal and determination as the decade before. If the answer is no, several of the recurring questions of life will need to be faced and answered with the leading one being, *Can I start again?*

Decade Five: The Forties. Evaluation.

The fortieth birthday is a great time for evaluating willingly or unwillingly life so far. If the evaluation is positive, the number of recurring questions will have eased. The constant looking ahead of the previous decades now changes to looking back and evaluating achievement, relationships, and personal growth with a view to making any necessary adjustments. **The actual self** being firmly **bonded** with **the imagined self** is a reliable indication that all is going well so far. If the evaluation is negative, the number of recurring questions will increase, and the demand for positive action will become insistent and prolonged. The highly destructive seed of regret can be sown during this time.

Decade Six: The Fifties. Consolidation.

Providing the previous decade's requirements have been met, the recurring questions of life will now pose an interesting challenge rather than a threat to well-being. This decade will be a time when strength and solidarity will aid relationships, health, financial stability, spiritual awareness, and personal development.

Decade Seven: The Sixties & Beyond. Contentment.

This is a wonderful time of life and can often be when materialistic thoughts and endeavors begin to wane, ultimately allowing the discovery of the more serene and uplifting pursuits of life that were overlooked or missed during the hurly burly of previous decades.

One recurring question can arise early in life and many times in every decade thereafter: *Should I fear the future?*

The 10-Year Glitch provides a blueprint for life with many practical examples and advice on ways to look forward to a positive future by eliminating problems from the past and enjoying every moment of the present.

The bulk of the book's contents are derived from personal growth, relationship, and motivation workshops; seminars; lectures; and counseling sessions the authors have conducted over the past twenty-five years.

Early chapters explore the many ways the recurring questions affect every facet of life, both positively and negatively. Final chapters are devoted to original motivation and personal growth techniques. They also include lessons that

Introducing the 10-Year Glitch

helped many people of all ages to obtain major improvements in their relationships, finances, and ability to change, as well as to discover their spiritual selves.

NOTE: A number of chapters appear to repeat subjects from previous chapters, but each chapter deals with the recurring subjects from a different angle and provides a good example of the book's theme of recurring trends and patterns.

The 10-Year Glitch

Chapter Two

No Better Time to Live

One of the more bewildering aspects of the earthly experience is the element known as time. Everyone gets twenty-four hours per day/night cycle, but it is not enough for some and too much for others.

Time is the great paradox. It can be both friend and foe, wasted and saved, found and lost, servant and master. It heals and hurts, can take ages to arrive yet be gone in a flash. It dictates, bullies, nurtures, and destroys. It supplies the beginning, middle, and end of every cycle, endeavor, event, performance, celebration, decade, and life span.

Although time as an entity is non-judgmental, as a sole arbiter, it punishes those who continually refuse to use it wisely and rewards those who appreciate its inestimable value and treat it with the reverence accorded to any great materialistic treasure.

Roman writer and philosopher Seneca captured the importance of time in our daily lives when he said, *"Hurry up and start living well with the thought that each day is a life unto itself."* A modern philosophy urges us to *"live in the now."* With such a barrage of commercial encouragement to plan, plan,

plan, for the future, it is easy to miss the enjoyment and health-promoting benefit of life and living in the now.

Time, as with everything else in the universe, is subject to the law of cause and effect. It is possible to enlist time as a lifelong ally, one capable of providing a loyal, harmonious companionship throughout each decade and the duration of a life span. For that to happen, it is necessary to accept and apply a number of uncompromising directions that time itself has created to ensure an orderly process between birth and death.

The first direction is not to dwell excessively in the past. There is nothing more frustrating or energy sapping than trying to patch up the past, wallowing in a long-gone disaster or tragedy, or pining moodily for what used to be. Today is far more relevant than yesterday!

Naturally, the second direction is not to spend an inordinate amount of time thinking about the future.

Should I fear the future?

As you will see in a number of upcoming chapters, the above question is triggered in many different ways. On almost every occasion, the subject of time is involved. A wise and easily overlooked philosophy states, *"The present inevitably becomes the future, so prepare for the future by doing everything right in the present."* In other words, there is no future, just a continuing present.

A proven method for preventing the erosion of present time is to use time as a motivating trigger for any aspect of personal growth and development. This technique is especially potent when used for New Year's resolutions, affirmations, or any other form of **self-talk** aimed at achieving a positive, and perhaps essential, change of attitude, belief, or inclination.

No Better Time to Live

The first step for using the powerful technique is to utter sincerely the words, *"It's time I ... "* and then add whatever it is time for. Obvious examples would include "... give up smoking (or any other health-threatening habit)," "... stop complaining about my life and instead make necessary changes to overcome the cause of the complaints," or "... forget the problems of the past and get on with living now." Using this proven, life-enhancing exercise, all of the seven recurring questions of life, which are listed below, can be successfully answered.

- Am I who I want to be?
- Should I feel guilty?
- Am I where I should be?
- When should I say it is over?
- Can I start again?
- What if I get it wrong?
- Should I fear the future?

It is vital to note and accept that trying to force something to happen before its time is the major reason for many good intentions or ardently desired aspirations failing to materialize. Time responds far more favorably to logic and planning than to pure emotion. An important decision based solely on emotion is usually what prompts people to force something to happen in their time rather than the time when emotion, logic, and planning are working together in harmony.

With the foregoing note of caution in mind, pause now for a few minutes and think about or write down one or more *"It's time I..."* statements. Once selected, a physical plan of action should be immediately implemented and sustained until the desired result is achieved. (Methods to achieve this are included in chapters nineteen and twenty-four.)

* * *

One life element that simply cannot be separated from time is the element of age. The time and age combination operates over a life span, and in turn, it is divided into decades. Each decade produces challenging, recurring questions requiring definite answers and actions within the decade they occur. Many, if not all, of life's frustrations and low points happen when the recurring questions and requirements of a particular decade are ignored or postponed.

Recurring questions are not an issue during pre-teen years because if any arise, parents, guardians, or some other external influence will deal with them. The teenage years consist of a high degree of dependence, although the teenager's desire for independence can cause friction and confusion when recurring questions arise, such as:

- Am I who I want to be?
- Am I where I should be?

The third and fourth decades (twenties and thirties age groups) are the years when time must be used *"to the nth degree."* They are the years in a life span for being time-selfish—an essential, health-enhancing prerequisite for a fast-paced, seemingly frantic lifestyle.

People differ in their attitudes regarding the value of time. Some believe in a time-selfish philosophy. As genuine strivers, they become devotees of time management strategies that allow them maximum use of time in an orderly, organized fashion. They seem to get so much done and to achieve so many things, but they never seem to be in a hurry.

No Better Time to Live

On the other hand, others imagine they are striving, but a closer look reveals that they are in fact time-abusers, skilled in the developed art of frittering time away. They use as camouflage the self-deluding, oft-repeated statement, "*I never seem to have enough time.*"

It is a destructive habit that, in the long term, can become a stress-inducing problem. Time controlling the individual is extremely counterproductive when compared to the individual controlling time. Lord Chesterfield, the eighteenth century writer and orator, could have been talking about the time-abuser when he said, "*The less one has to do the less time one finds to do it in.*"

There are many old sayings relating to time: "*Time waits for no man,*" "*time on my hands,*" and a puzzling one that states, "*Time is a postulate.*" Upon consulting a dictionary, one learns that this saying can mean that time is a demand, a necessary condition, and that time is taken for granted, but it is also meaningless.

This makes a little more sense when we realize that time is only related to the planet Earth and exists nowhere else in the universe. Time on earth is a puzzle, as there are so many different time zones. It is one time on one side of the world and another time on the other. Even in the same country, different time zones exist, making the element of time quite meaningless.

Metaphysically, we are told there is no time, because past, present, and future are all one. There is only the now, and every event throughout the universe is happening at the same time. This is a hard one for us humans to get our heads around, but it can be likened to the following example. When one goes to a movie theater complex, several movies are being run simultaneously. We can only view the movies one at a time, although they are in fact all being shown at the same time.

However, if we were placed above the theatre, and we could remove the roof, we would be able to see all films at the same time. This is what is happening with our past, present, and future; they are all running at the same time. The phenomenon has been described as follows: *"Time is just a cosmic convenience that prevents everything from happening at once."*

* * *

It is said that when it is time for you to die, you will do so whether you want to go or not. Therefore, is death considered fate or a pre-appointed time set down and agreed to by our soul before we even began our life's journey? Here are some dark and macabre stories that make one think that when it is time, you go, and when it is not, you do not!

A filmmaker was making a movie on the dangers of low-level bridges when the truck on which he was standing passed under a low-level bridge, killing him. It was time.

A factory owner narrowly escaped death when a windblast flattened his factory except for one wall. After treatment for minor injuries, he returned to the scene to search for files. The remaining wall then collapsed and killed him. It was time.

A depressed man who could not find a job sat in his kitchen with a gun in his hand, threatening to kill himself. His wife pleaded with him not to do it, and after an hour, he burst into tears. He threw the gun to the floor. It went off and killed his wife. It was obviously his wife's time rather than his own.

A burglar was disturbed during a robbery and fled out the back door. He clambered over a nine-foot wall, dropped down, and found himself in the city prison. It was time to face the consequences of his deeds.

* * *

Am I who I want to be?

This one recurring question also provides a repetitive challenge during the striving decades. Because of the time and effort required to maintain the striving, it is easy to lose touch with the true self and become whatever other people want you to be.

Since the twenties and thirties are a time of great transition, with a host of new skills to learn in a wide variety of areas that require a dramatic increase in responsibilities, it can very easily lead to attempts at being all things to all people. Regardless of whether these attempts occur within an occupation, parenting, other relationships, or the social realm, the result can be the stunting of personal growth and personality that in later years is the root cause of deep-seated regret.

Am I where I should be?

The fifth decade (forties age group) is the decade for evaluation. This is an obvious and essential recurring question requiring an honest, courageous analysis of the striving years. This decade has become the "danger decade" for many reasons. Allowing the decade to get under way without any attempt at evaluation can, and often does, condemn the decade to a continuation of striving. Much of it will prove unnecessary, being more a force of habit rather than a productive enterprise.

The evaluation decade is the perfect time to decide if what you have achieved to this date is really what you wanted. The appraisal should cover numerous life facets, including work, relationships, social, and personal. If all facets are in harmony, the recurring question requires no answer. If, however, one or more facet is causing escalating problems, two serious recurring questions will arise.

When should I say it is over?

Can I start again?

The beginning of this decade is the perfect time to check your direction and ultimate destination. The decade has a built-in appraisal check, known as *"the big 4-0."* People who fear their fortieth birthday do so because of a real or perceived feeling that dreams, goals, or aspirations have not been fulfilled due to having made less than an all-out effort during the striving decades. It is also the time when problems from wrong, irrational, or irresponsible choices are magnified.

This is a time when the **tumble dryer mind** condition (detailed in chapter twenty-one) can start endlessly churning worry and anxious thoughts about, making it difficult to concentrate on seeking a solution. The sinking feeling of it now being too late to alter, change, or eliminate makes the idea of an honest, courageous evaluation seem too painful to contemplate. It is a ready-made time for negative mood swings and bouts of depression.

However, time reveals its benevolent side by providing an escape clause to alleviate this situation. Knowing that *"it's never too late"* is a lifeline available to anyone willing to shout a resounding "yes" to the recurring question: *Can I start again?*

Regardless of the area to which the question refers, it will take a high degree of courage to decide it is possible and desirable to correct the offending choice and make a fresh start. Many a life has been reduced to one of a submissive quality because the early forties evaluation was either done in a careless, thoughtless way or, far worse, was not done at all in the hope that the universe or some other outside agency such as fate or prayer would rescue the situation. This is usually a vain hope.

Starting again is often far easier than imagined, because it does have the powerful element of experience, a priceless element not available the first time around.

Consolidation is the role played during the sixth decade, the fifties age group.

Now is the **time** to bring together all that is considered valuable, important, and otherwise vital for maintaining a harmonious, healthy spiritual and earthly existence. If done for the right reasons, a superior quality-of-life bond is created—a bond that will provide many benefits for the following decades.

Unfortunately, the bond will not form if the frantic, unnecessary striving is still at full pace and the evaluation has been totally ignored. When that happens, the consolidation decade becomes one of utter confusion. The three elements of striving, evaluation, and consolidation all merge in a mishmash, creating a constant, unrelenting barrage of problems. Not only does this cause a highly stress-inducing existence, it also creates apprehension for the transition into the next decade.

The seventh decade, the sixties age group and onwards, is quite rightly known as the contentment decade.

It is **time** to reap the rewards of good planning, positive thinking, and courageous actions when confronted by any of the seven recurring questions. It is also **time** for the intelligent application of many of the principles and philosophies recorded throughout this book.

Certainly, there are still opportunities and health-promoting reasons for some striving, evaluation, and consolidation, but it is done in a relaxed, stress-free way, which also typifies the true meaning of contentment: *Satisfaction of one's desires fully.*

The 10-Year Glitch

As stated previously, regardless of which decade a person is in, one recurring question can be the most difficult to answer.

Should I fear the future?

Respecting time and its incessant, but fair, demands is one way of avoiding the devastating physical and mental state of fearing the future. *When there is no fear of the future, there is no better time to live!*

Chapter Three

The Risky Business Called Change

Making a change in one's life is viewed as a challenge by some and as a threat by others. The key to deciding whether the change is warranted or desirable is to ask if not making the change will cause a major regret in a later decade.

One of the more telling comments about life is that nothing is more permanent than change. It is a dominant player in every decade and usually the resolution to every one of the recurring questions of life.

Is change inevitable? Doesn't every day hold the challenge of the unknown, making each one different from the last in some respect?

Whenever thoughts about making a life-altering change are contemplated, a mind function known as **self-doubt** will immediately supply a seemingly endless supply of negative reasons why the change is an unwise decision. The first doubt will be triggered by the thought, *"What will my relatives or friends say if I change?"*

The 10-Year Glitch

Self-doubt ensures that change of virtually any description does not come easily or quickly. It is a cunning foe waiting to strike at the most vulnerable moments, and it is extremely adept at undermining dreams, goals, ideas, and aspirations. Therefore, the mind condition of self-doubt should never be underestimated or dismissed as easy to overcome.

Self-doubt draws much of its influence from the memory, especially memories of past failures, negative influences, inappropriate role models, or persistent criticism of self-expression. It is a permanent part of the human psyche, a fact than can be proven by simply taking self-confident people out of their areas of expertise and putting them into foreign environments in which they have no skill or knowledge.

Self-doubt relies on fear of the future and, therefore, the unknown for many of its doom-laden messages. Once understood, it can be brought under control and used as a motivational ally rather than a destructive, negative enemy.

However, being unaware of self-doubt's capacity for eroding even the most emotional and logically sound decision is the major reason why many fail to achieve what they most ardently desire. They can become constantly thwarted in their quest for a meaningful purpose in their lives.

The fear of public speaking is an obvious demonstration of self-doubt in action. Learning and applying techniques aimed at relegating self-doubt to a minor, almost non-existent role can overcome that particular fear.

To achieve a similar triumph in day-to-day life, it is essential to accept the challenge of change when the need for change is irrevocably obvious. The more times the challenge is accepted, the less self-doubt can influence decision making. Conversely, the more a person rejects change when it should be made, the more he or she becomes a victim of self-doubt. The result becomes a life lived in virtual limbo.

The Risky Business Called Change

The need for change is not exclusively a self-deciding issue. In ever-increasing instances, change is being forced upon people both with and without warning. A life-enhancing key to survival in today's fast moving, fickle, quickly changing environment is to see the need for change beforehand rather than when it becomes unavoidable.

Life-long regrets often flow from the moment people refuse or fail to commit themselves to making a glaringly obvious change! Relationships of all types are an area that provides many glaringly obvious needs for change, but it is also the most common area for delaying, avoiding, or simply refusing to accept the inevitable. The common denominator for long-married couples is that they are willing to make the change.

When a change is obviously needed in a two-person relationship, an equal contribution from both partners is required in order to succeed. A crisis soon arises when one partner in a counseling session is adamant he or she is not at fault and therefore does not need to make any changes. *"That's the way I am, and I can't change!"* is often the mantra of a person who will prove to be extremely difficult in any type of relationship.

One kind of change that needs to be avoided is change for the sake of change. Disaster usually follows any decision to force a change based predominantly on emotions with very little or no regard for logic. When there is a lack of a genuine reason for the change, and it is more a whim decision with the idea of finding greener pastures, the change becomes a major mistake if the pastures prove meaner rather than greener.

A definite obstacle to overcome when considering change is the fear of failure. The recurring question triggering the fear is: *What if I get it wrong?*

Provided the change is based on sound reasoning, the fear of making a mistake is unfortunate and usually unwarranted

The 10-Year Glitch

because it is a fear of the future. Of all life's fears, fear of the future is perhaps the most debilitating because nothing can be done about it until the future becomes the present.

It is surely a perverse act to fear something that cannot be touched when humans have been given any number of ways to control, influence, and guide their present lives. One extremely powerful way is the universal law that states, *The physical body cannot react to two thoughts at the same time.* You can think, walk, or run and do one or the other, because you cannot do both at the same time! You can think yes or no, can or cannot, will or will not, but a definite choice has to be made between the two options before physical action can take place.

Like so many universal laws, this one is deceptively simple, but those who blame anything or anyone when things go wrong, or do not go according to plan, do not adhere to it. The inescapable truth is that all of us were given the ability to choose a course of action. That, in turn, means accepting full responsibility for all reactions resulting from that choice!

The ability to choose begets the ability to change. The simple expression, *"I've changed my mind"* demonstrates the ability to choose between two courses of action.

Once the foregoing universal law is understood, the negative influence of self-doubt can be reduced to an easily managed level. Once this is achieved, the way is open for the law to be used in a positive, mind-enhancing manner.

Generally speaking, and providing there is no medical problem, when a person is feeling down in mental or physical energy or enthusiasm, it can often be traced to a single, negatively based thought circling endlessly around in the mind. Until the reason for the thought is identified and subsequent action taken to confront and eliminate the cause, it will continue its damaging effect on mind and body.

The Risky Business Called Change

If the cause cannot be readily confronted within the immediate future, then the negative influence of the malignant thought can be downgraded and often negated by substituting an uplifting, positive thought. Witness the effect on a person when given good news. The reaction is an instant, uplifting, positive boost to both mind and body, regardless of the mental or physical condition at the time of receiving the news. The mind immediately reacts to the new, single-thought injection.

Naturally, bad news creates the opposite effect. A person feeling good before receiving the bad news instantly feels morose; someone feeling down before receiving bad news sinks further into moroseness. A doctor can either elevate or plunge the spirits of a patient with a good or bad prognosis.

The moral of the examples is that if an external suggestion can affect a mental and physical condition so quickly, then an internal or self-prompting suggestion will achieve the same effect. Think good or bad, because you cannot have both at the same time.

One of the surest ways to utilize the **one-thought technique** in order to achieve a good, health-enhancing mental state is through the proven method of positive affirmations.

Affirmations work on a number of subtle levels, but their real value lies in the ability to give a dream, a prayer, or a wish a **symbolic bridge** from the present to the future! It does that by using a remarkable mind function known as **visualization**, the ability to see in the mind's eye the outcome of an event before it has happened.

With ever-increasing study and research into the impressive scope of visualization, it appears this function will provide the link between the finite mind of humans and infinite intelligence. It is beginning to reveal the process by which mental impulses are modified and changed into their spiritual equivalent.

In a number of medical circles, the visualization process is gaining increasing acceptance, with imagination being a key and contributing element. Psychic and clairvoyant abilities are other areas with visualization connections.

In everyday life, visualization can be used as a technique for aiding decision making. The difficulty created by change for many people is that they cannot see an alternative solution, so they ultimately succumb to a meek decision to do nothing and put up with the unsatisfactory situation. Using visualization to picture the result a change would create, removes the fear of the unknown, the fear that feeds self-doubt.

The natural enemy of self-doubt is belief. Belief starts to flourish when a decision to change is accepted as an exciting, life-enhancing challenge.

In metaphysical circles, the color orange is thought to be marvelous for eradicating fear and encouraging self-confidence. The color orange can also help to give character trait stability, aid the stimulation and assimilation of new ideas, and bring a sense of freedom from limitations. So if you are about to face the challenge of change, be daring. Wear something orange, or carry a citrine crystal or a piece of amber on your person, and feel the orange energies bringing positive changes to your mental and emotional outlook.

Also, boost your confidence by listening to music that has the same vibration frequency as the color orange. Suggestions include *Hungarian Dance Number 5* by Brahms, "Habanera" from *Carmen* by Bizet, or "Jupiter" from *The Planets* by Holst.

When considering change, be secure in the knowledge that our soul never undertakes anything that we cannot handle. At a deeper level, we are undertaking an experience that will ultimately lead to our universal growth and maturity.

CHAPTER FOUR

Tolerance—The Second Great Virtue

Tolerance of other people's shortcomings is one sure way of achieving a non-confrontational and harmonious relationship. The following story serves as an introduction to this chapter's subject.

Lucas Potter was a contented fifty-two-year-old bachelor who lived with his parents right up until they died within a year of each other.

Lucas had three dominant character traits: conscientiousness, dependability, and predictability. Although considered a boring trio of traits by many Baby Boomers, they were nevertheless highly suited to his public service job with a government information analysis department.

Each day, Lucas would sift through thousands of pieces of information (collected by a variety of other government departments) in the vain hope of finding something remotely useful, constructive, or beneficial to man or womankind.

The 10-Year Glitch

Away from the workplace, Lucas's great enjoyment in life stemmed from, and was generated by, an uninhibited penchant for singing (around the home), whistling (while playing ball with his dog), and humming (when shopping at the supermarket).

Lucas did appreciate and accept his musical limitations. However, it did not stop him from having an ambitious repertoire, which included light opera, country & western, and traditional English folk songs.

Karaoke Night at the local hotel failed to interest Lucas, as he did not choose to inflict his dubious talent on the hotel's patrons. It was a sentiment that many hotel patrons wished some of the regular karaoke performers would adopt.

Lucas did have one exciting social outlet in his life, and that was a weekly session at a ballroom dancing school. Being an eligible bachelor, and much admired for his impressive fandango, Lucas was a popular selection during ladies-choose-your-partner time. However, apart from that female contact, Lucas seemed to be quite happy to live life as an unattached male, unconsciously avoiding the subtle innuendoes and ploys of unattached females.

The apparent lack of interest in the opposite sex naturally triggered rumors, but such was his vibrant, manly, testosterone-driven dancing that no one took the rumors seriously.

One day, a new member joined the dancing school. Her name was Henrietta Clay. She was a striking woman, tall and imposing of stature, with a commanding presence that demanded attention, respect, and perhaps a bit of cowering from timid people.

It was not surprising to learn that Henrietta had been an opera singer of some note before retiring to pursue a teaching career. She was also a singing eisteddfod adjudicator much feared by contestants due to her obsession for clarity of phrase and preciseness of intonation and performance.

Tolerance—The Second Great Virtue

Somehow, the strange, unfathomable laws of romance conspired to draw Lucas and Henrietta together. Within months, via many a waltz, quickstep, foxtrot, and steamy, body-grinding Latin American selection, the romance blossomed to the point where marriage was contemplated and ultimately agreed upon.

Following a dignified wedding ceremony and a two-week dignified honeymoon, both of which added a degree of dignity to the relationship, Lucas and Henrietta settled into what they anticipated would be a life of dignified wedded bliss.

A few weeks into married life, Lucas was standing in the shower stall when it occurred to him that since his relationship with Henrietta began, he had ceased singing, whistling, and humming because of all the new, exciting experiences. He immediately set about correcting the situation by performing a sensitive rendition of "I Got Plenty O' Nuttin'" from his favorite light opera, Porgy and Bess.

Halfway through, and at a point when Lucas was approaching full, vibrant voice, a series of loud staccato raps on the bathroom door curtailed the vocal rendering.

"Darling, that rendition is too con affeto," Henrietta Clay-Potter called out. "George Gershwin scored it for either con brio or con fuoco."

She then demonstrated what she meant in a powerful, strident voice that rattled the contents of the bathroom cabinet and caused the Alka Seltzer to start fizzing in its bottle. Lucas was utterly bemused, bothered, and bewildered, and he decided to pull the shower curtain closed on his performance.

Later that same day, Lucas was in the garden combining two of his favorite pleasures--playing ball with Jock the Scottish terrier and whistling country & western songs from the CD Mournful, Meaningless, and Meandering. Suddenly, Henrietta called out in a chastising tone from a window in the house.

The 10-Year Glitch

"*Darling, your pitch in the upper register is a semitone too high.*"

She then demonstrated what she meant with a piercing whistle that caused Jock to fall over when he tried to cover his ears with his front paws. The window closed, leaving Lucas utterly confused and, much as he tried to avoid it, slightly irritated.

Several days later, Lucas and Henrietta went shopping together for the first time. They were walking down the refrigerated foods aisle when Lucas received yet another technical admonishment alongside the butter and margarine section.

As he merrily hummed a version of his favorite traditional English folk song, "O'er Yon Meadowlea," Henrietta murmured, "Darling, take a lot more care with your portamento.*"*

She then demonstrated the skill of carrying the sound in a continuous slide from one note to another by humming a piece from Pietro Mascagni's one-act opera, Cavalleria Rusticana. *The degree of technical excellence left Lucas utterly flabbergasted and, much as he once again tried to avoid it, decidedly resentful!*

During the next few weeks, Lucas Potter's every attempt to sing, whistle, or hum was constantly cut short and otherwise thwarted by unsolicited advice and constructive criticism.

Jock was the first to notice his master's despondent mood and the absence of the whistling accompaniment to the ball chasing. He even attempted to cheer his master up by barking a few of the C&W hits he had heard so often. Apart from attracting the amorous attention of a music-loving Labrador, however, Jock's efforts failed to lift his master's spirits.

Everyone in the neighborhood noticed the change in the nice, happy-go-lucky Mr. Potter, and all agreed he did not seem to be himself since marrying "that strange woman."

At the office, a distracted Lucas suddenly began to glean useful snippets of information from the incoming mountain of paperwork. This infuriated his superiors, because instead of feeding the paper shredder non-stop, they were forced to make decisions and write reports—two highly dangerous, career-threatening exercises in any government department!

*Henrietta was the next to notice the change, so she asked if there was anything wrong and if she could help. Lucas should have immediately accepted the offer. Being unaware of the importance of **communication** in a happy marriage, and not wishing to upset Henrietta at this point in their relationship, he declined to reveal the reason for his melancholy mood.*

*However, people who practice the second great virtue can only shake their heads in sympathy for Lucas Potter's plight. Although patience is the first great virtue, relationships can be greatly enriched by the second great virtue known as tolerance, especially when applied to **being tolerant of other people's shortcomings!***

How do you react to other people's shortcomings or general behavior?

Record a number indicating your tolerance level for each category using a scale of 1 to 10 as defined below.

0 to 3 is *little or no reaction* and may mean you are overly tolerant to the point that other people take advantage of you or lack respect for you. The expression *"suffering in silence"* aptly describes the condition. Ultimately, resentment sets in, and quality of life deteriorates.

7 to 10 indicates an *over-reaction and a lack of tolerance* that often leads to rage in the 9 and 10 levels.

4, 5, or 6 are the *ideal response* figures, inasmuch as they allow a reasonable amount of tolerance. When your tolerance level is exceeded, it is made known to the offender.

The 10-Year Glitch

The main areas of tolerance testing include:

Forgetfulness
A tolerance level can be severely tested when other people forget an event that one person considers important enough to be remembered. _____

Irritating habits
Because humans as a rule are habit-driven, it is certain that in a relationship, one person's habit(s) can be another person's irritation(s). _____

Idiosyncrasies
Some people develop these peculiar or different ways of doing things as part of their personality. Because it is not *"the way we do things,"* it requires a degree of tolerance in allowing and accepting idiosyncratic behavior. _____

Criticism
As portrayed in the Lucas Potter story, constant criticism is so powerful it can change another person's personality. Criticism is actually an affirmation working in the autosuggestion area and, therefore, should not be tolerated too long before applying 4, 5, or 6 to nip it in the bud. Careful thought should also be given to **constructive criticism** because it so easily becomes **destructive criticism**. _____

Punctuality

Knowing a person who is always late for everything requires a degree of tolerance up to the point when the aberration becomes an irritation requiring 4, 5, or 6 attention. _____

Rage

Rage includes any of the types now so prevalent in this modern, frantic, get-out-of-my-way-I'm-in-a-hurry world. Road rage is the most common and dangerous rage with sometimes dire repercussions. It is the area in which tolerance should be practiced and applied at all times, with no excuse for allowing the tolerance level to reach the 9 and 10 marks. This is perhaps the only time when a tolerance level of 0 to 3 can be an advantage. An attitude of allowing selfish, careless, law-breaking, and plain stupid drivers to flash in and out of your life for a split second without being overly tolerance-challenged is an intelligent way to avoid road rage confrontation. _____

Now add up your answers for all of the tolerance testers. How did you score? A well-balanced, tolerant person will score between 24 and 36.

The final part of this tolerance exercise is to ask the following question: *How tolerant do other people have to be of you in one or more of the above categories?*

The 10-Year Glitch

CHAPTER FIVE

Am I Who I Want to Be?

Since the dawn of civilization, the subject of relationships has provided a topic for discussion and dissection. Television, radio, magazines, books, theater, and movies, together with a host of other outlets, all develop their volume of outpourings from the rich, but almost unfathomable complexity, associated with relationships.

That *"No man (or woman) is an island"* is graphically illustrated when we realize how many diverse relationships both become involved in during a lifetime. Apart from the basic family, friends, social, sport, and work relationships, most of which are by choice, financial, legal, and bureaucratic relationships are often unavoidable aspects of life.

Any relationship can be good, bad, or indifferent. It can be peaceful or warring, loving or loathing, friction-free or harshly grating, life-enhancing or life-threatening. However, as varied and disparate as relationships can be, a common denominator is a make-or-break element in any relationship. People are the common denominator!

- *People create the complexity present in relationships.*
- *People inject into a relationship the love, caring, honesty, and many other virtues that make a harmonious relationship one of the truly great pleasures of the earthly experience.*
- *People also inject the bitterness, hate, dishonesty, selfishness, and many other personality aberrations that break a relationship and cause it to be one of the truly intolerable displeasures of the earthly experience.*

To unravel the reason for relationships developing complications, it is essential to examine the relationship with **self**. It is a relationship more bewildering, infuriating, elusive, and elaborate than one between two or more people.

Until the relationship with self is secure and comfortable, it is highly probable that tensions and pressures will dominate any type of relationship with others. To achieve the self-confidence that flows from knowing *"what makes you tick"* most of the time, it is necessary to be aware of a basic but vital mind function called **character traits**.

Character traits, also known as personality traits, supply the answers to the following recurring question and its companion sub question: *Am I who I want to be? Am I prepared to reveal it to the world?*

The physical body relies on a healthy character trait balance for its continued well-being. The widespread scope and influence of character traits can be judged and appreciated from the following sample list.

Although the list is condensed, one hundred or so character analysis workshops identified the selected traits as being a reliable, widespread, cross section representation.

Am I Who I Want to Be?

Positive character traits include:	**Negative** character traits include:
Proud	Arrogant
Loyal	Cynical
Trusting	Deceitful
Cooperative	Unpredictable
Creative	Dishonest
Dependable	Derisive
Intuitive	Tactless
Passionate	Conceited
Determined	Changeable
Idealistic	Hypocritical
Faithful	Insensitive
Enthusiastic	Introverted
Agreeable	Offensive
Sensitive	Moody
Patient	Reckless
Charismatic	Possessive
Dignified	Stubborn
Diplomatic	Timid
Extrovert	Suspicious
Stable	Sarcastic
Open-minded	Indecisive
Curious	Irresponsible
Conscientious	Secretive
Levelheaded	Judgmental
Industrious	Impulsive

The 10-Year Glitch

Sensitive	Egotistical
Ambitious	Complacent
Visionary	Obsessive
Optimistic	Pessimistic

The two lists give you some idea of why relationships can be so complex and complicated when the above mix-and-match traits come together in a relationship situation. However, a general rule prevents relationships from becoming unworkable because of too many conflicting character traits. The majority of people function with two or three **dominant positive** character traits and two or three **dominant negative** character traits.

The key word is **dominant**. Additional traits surface from time to time to assist in an unusual situation, but for the most part, life is driven by a balanced fluctuation between the two or three positive and negative traits.

Before offering examples that substantiate the foregoing theory, it is important to appreciate that without character traits there would be no books, movies, television shows, plays, videos, or any other literary work that relies on fiction for its dramatic or comic existence.

Reading or watching a work of fiction triggers a mind function called **empathy**, the ability to project and identify with another person's thoughts and feelings by comparing them with one's own experiences.

Recall the last time you laughed, cried, loved, loathed, cheered, booed, or felt inspired or crushed by the behavior of a character in a work of fiction. Great fiction of any kind usually features memorable characters with clearly defined character traits. A number of character trait clichés provide an insight into the subject.

Am I Who I Want to Be?

You are your own worst enemy means that every time a person tries to do something worthy with the thrust of a positive trait, a negative trait proves to be stronger and thwarts the attempt. If it happens too many times, a negative comfort zone is established. As a result, the positive traits become non-functional, and the oft-repeated phrase "*Why is this happening again?*" is a natural by-product of the condition.

Acting out of character occurs when a submerged negative trait suddenly surfaces as an impulsive thought or action and short-circuits the established positive character traits. An example would be the honest, trustworthy professional who begins to gamble with clients' funds and allows the negative trait to create a web of deception, leading to long-term embezzlement. Another example would be a normally indecisive, timid person who becomes a brave hero when confronted with a real-life situation that demands instant action in order to save a life. For the duration of the event, positive character traits push aside the normal negative traits.

A technique used by fiction writers is to put characters in situations that are alien to their character traits—the square peg in a round hole premise. For many people, that same premise is the major cause for most of life's complications and dramas due to **character trait confusion**.

The confusion is often started at a young age. Children displaying an outgoing, extroverted trait are told to *"stop showing off."* A curious, articulate child is told to *"stop asking so many questions."*

During the teenage years, when a constant search for identity takes place, the opportunity to supply a positive answer to the recurring question, *Am I who I want to be?* is often thwarted by well-meaning adults or peer pressure, resulting once again in character trait confusion.

Poor choices and bad decisions are two of the more destructive outcomes arising from the inability of young adults to determine their personal character traits. Not accepting, understanding, acknowledging, or knowing the role played by character traits can be the cause for unpalatable **repeating patterns** and bouts of confusion throughout a lifetime. Relationships with self and others are constantly under pressure because of the confusion.

Positive character traits supply the drive and motivation for the achievement of goals, ambitions, hopes, and dreams, which provide new and exciting challenges and outlets for personal growth. Negative character traits supply the self-doubt and fear of change that slow down some and completely stop others.

The starting point for appreciating character trait function is the acceptance that two selves reside within the psyche.

1. *The imagined self*—a future projection.
2. *The actual self*—a present reality.

The imagined self mentally creates the result of a person's aspiration, dream, or desire and is a good example of visualization in action.

- *"This is something I used to dream would happen" is the statement most often uttered by award recipients.*
- *That nothing happens by accident is a clue about the projection thinking capabilities of the imagined self.*

Inventors and visionaries use the imagined self to see into the future virtually to produce something in the present. The absence of imagined self-thinking can mean the lack of any kind of future expectations. It can also mean being "stuck in a rut" and being content to stay there. The actual self is the precommitment self, excited, yet apprehensive, about the task set by the imagined self. There is a gap between the two selves.

The size of the gap is in direct proportion to the size and scope of the dream.

While the gap remains, goals, dreams, desires, and ambitions will prove to be as elusive as a sleep-related dream. Success in any form happens when the gap is bridged, allowing the two selves to bond and become an inseparable unit dedicated to a common cause. Essential positive character traits required to achieve the bonding would include at least two of the following:

- *Enthusiastic*
- *Persistent*
- *Industrious*
- *Honest*
- *Conscientious*
- *Decisive*
- *Determined*

Negative character traits that would hinder the bonding would include the negative opposite of these positive traits, along with liberal doses of **procrastination.**

Procrastination is not in and of itself a character trait but rather the by-product of one or more genuine negative character traits producing mental laziness. Procrastination is accurately described as *"the thief of time"* and is an extremely destructive mind function, because it stifles potential, stunts talent, and feeds the inability to get things done when they should be done.

The 10-Year Glitch

Any discussion dealing with relationships, of course, would be incomplete if it did not include the relationship of marriage in its deliberations. Marriage, the major person-to-person commitment, is also the severest examination of the imagined/actual self and positive/negative character trait relationship. Worldwide concern about the continually soaring divorce rate indicates too many couples are failing the examination, resulting in an escalation of the family unit breakdown.

The role played by character traits in the marriage relationship is, in many respects, similar to their function in other relationships such as:

- *Parent-child*
- *Teacher-pupil*
- *Employer-employee*
- *Same-sex and opposite-sex friendships*
- *Any type of relationship where two people desire to interact in a harmonious manner*

There must be **give and take** in reasonably equal proportions.

There must be allowances for compromise, cooperation, and character trait flexibility.

There must be a willingness to learn, adjust, change, forgive, and forget.

Above all, there must be a generous degree of **tolerance!**

The following three "aspects of marriage" illustrate why, as stated in some marriage vows, *"for better or for worse"* is an early warning about the mix-and-match of character traits.

Aspect One: The Fantasy Version

Two people meet and start a meaningful relationship.

The physical chemistry is perfect.

During the early communication exchanges, each fully and frankly reveals both his/her dominant positive and negative character traits.

The character traits are a compatible match, meaning the mental chemistry is perfect.

They get married.

The physical and mental chemistry remain at their perfect levels for the rest of their long married life.

They live happily ever after without once needing to make any kind of adjustment or change, and therefore there was no need for a generous degree of **tolerance**.

Aspect Two: The Reality Version (in too Many Cases)

Two people meet and start a meaningful relationship.

The physical chemistry is perfect.

During the early communication exchanges, each display and promote their positive character traits while doing everything possible to hide or otherwise camouflage their negative character traits.

The mental chemistry *appears* to be perfect.

They get married.

Before too long, the real people emerge via the hitherto hidden negative character traits.

The 10-Year Glitch

His practical, strong-willed, optimistic positive character traits clash with her unpredictable, stubborn, pessimistic negative character traits.

Her outgoing, free-spirited, gregarious positive traits clash with his possessive, suspicious, insular negative traits.

What originally were minor habit variations that a generous degree of mutual *tolerance* could have overcome instead slowly and surely become seemingly insurmountable differences:

- He squeezes their shared toothpaste tube from the top…
- She squeezes the tube from the bottom….
- He would like to stay home more often…
- She would like to go out more often…
- He sees a hug as a prelude to sex…
- She sees a hug as a spur-of-the-moment, unconditional sign of affection…

Angry words, accusations, and personal jibes become the main form of communication.

The physical chemistry wanes dramatically.

He begins to enjoy regular drinking sessions at home with the television as a companion.

She begins to enjoy regular evenings out with her female friends.

Eventually, a trial separation is attempted….

It fails.

They become a divorce-rate statistic and still, to this day, neither fully understands what went wrong!

Aspect Three: The Ideal

One definition of ideal states: *"answering to one's highest conception, perfect, existing only in an idea."* Therefore, the ideal marriage or relationship begins as the same embryo from which every other man-made achievement has evolved—an idea. Most people enter into any kind of relationship with the idea that it will be ideal. The problem is that an idea is an abstract, and if nothing is added to give it life, it remains as ineffectual as an unopened present.

It is said that imagination is more important than knowledge. Imagination, coupled with an idea, is an ideal partnership that can be further enhanced with the addition of character trait attributes such as cooperation, patience, trusting, caring, and tolerance. When those attributes are incorporated within a marriage or other relationship, they will achieve as close to the ideal state as can be expected.

Prior to achieving the ideal state, a universal psychological truth must be accepted.

People who cannot or will not accept their positive and negative selves will experience difficulties accepting the positive and negative selves of others.

The first step in correcting that situation is to practice the life-enhancing, positive character trait known as tolerance. From many workshop questionnaires on the subject of character traits, three traits headed the list in their categories.

The 10-Year Glitch

1. *Optimism was voted the most influential positive character trait.*
2. *Pessimism was voted the most destructive negative character trait.*
3. *Tolerance was voted the one most likely to encourage relationship harmony.*

CHAPTER SIX

Feeling at Home With the Family

For some people, the family is the be all and end all of a lifetime earthly experience.

Nothing is too good, too much, or too anything if a member of the family is involved.

On the surface, that kind of closeness appears to provide a positive family environment. For many families considered by society to be happy families, the closeness does indeed create the source from which a long-lasting, harmonious relationship develops. For other people, the family is a source of constant irritation that often escalates into major conflicts, resulting in what is now known as a **dysfunctional family environment**.

For such a family, closeness represents a claustrophobia-type state. The desire to get away from the family confines and restrictions is a contributing reason for outbreaks of conflict, along with the nagging recurring question: *Am I where I should be?*

What are the factors causing such contrasting family environments? This question has spawned all manner of experts and organizations, all of which are attempting to reverse what is seen as a breakdown in the historical interpretation of the family unit.

That the family unit is no different from any other kind of relationship involving two or more people is one obvious answer to the breakdown question. All such relationships are subject to a regular, volatile mixture of character trait clashes, attitude attacks, power games, mood swings, and inflated egos, along with liberal doses of anger, jealousy, envy, and frustrations of all kinds. In fact, whatever one perceives as being right or wrong with the world, is generally the distinguishing element for what is right or wrong with the family unit. There is an ongoing debate about what constitutes a family unit according to government and societal bodies and interest groups.

1. *Is a single mother with a child a family unit?*
2. *Is a same-sex couple with an adopted child a family unit?*
3. *Is it essential that a child have both a male and female parent (father and mother) before the three-way union can be deemed a family unit?*

As the debate rages and the rules and regulations require constant scrutiny, the following current social event is sure to have repercussions in the not-too-distant future. An ever-increasing number of young, single females are having a baby without caring whether the child's father becomes part of the ongoing relationship. In many instances, the father is well and truly discouraged from additional involvement. Social workers are becoming alarmingly aware that many of these young women are simply providing themselves with a short-term solution to avoid life's early challenges rather than having any genuine maternal instincts.

Feeling at Home With the Family

The family unit subject takes a complicated twist when a relationship is started between two divorced people, both with children, who then add to the equation by having a child together. Known as the blended family unit, it can provide some unusual situations such as the one acted out in an inner-city schoolyard.

One young boy said to another, "If you punch me, I'll tell my dad."

The other boy replied, "Don't be stupid; your dad is also my dad!"

Critics of the one-parent family unit, of course, should be aware that one loving, caring, attentive parent is better than two parents are where one or the other is incapable or disinterested in giving the child anything resembling positive emotional benefits. Without doubt, a parent or parents who devote time and energy to being positive role models for their children will go a long way toward ensuring those same attributes will be passed on to future generations by way of a **positive hereditary character trait.** Conversely, children growing up in a family where little or no effort is made in demonstrating traditional values can often develop a **negative hereditary character trait.**

The hereditary factor is an important element in explaining why some families exist in harmony while others exist in a state of disharmony. A medical term for physical hereditary conditions is **familial** or **genetic,** and it refers to a **characteristic** or **disorder** that runs in the family. Male pattern baldness is an example of a familial characteristic, while hyperlipidemia (abnormally high levels of fat in the blood) is an example of a familial disorder.

Medical literature detailing reference material about familial factors makes no mention of inherited character traits. Being a condition of the mind, it cannot be treated by

The 10-Year Glitch

traditional medical means, and it is therefore dismissed as yet another all-in-the-mind aberration. However, any anti-social behavior or mental abuse observed and experienced during formative years will more than likely resurface in the form of a hereditary condition to be inflicted once more on a new generation.

Family therapy is one field deriving most of its work from the inherited character trait.

The need for this type of therapy became glaringly apparent when the historical family structure was fragmented with the arrival of the Baby Boomer generation, whose members were born between 1946 and 1964. The Baby Boomers were responsible for many social changes and upheavals, which were not always met with approval by the preceding generations.

However, the generation following the Baby Boomers is full of praise for the technological advances both developed and fast-tracked at the peak of the Baby Boomer period.

Two far-reaching influences were the birth of the career woman and the reluctance of career couples to start a family before obtaining the trappings of prosperity. Another Baby Boomer happening was the sophisticated development of the *"buy now, pay later"* credit-card mentality, which led to a massive increase in the national debt, a massive drop in personal savings, and the 1980s being labeled the decade of money-madness greed.

A good example of inherited character traits occurred with the children of Baby Boomers. It coincided with the creation of designer label products that cost many times more than the ordinary products devoid of a famous brand name or recognizable logo. A new kind of peer pressure was added to the family unit and income. Children simply had to have the latest fad or fashion, regardless of expense; otherwise, they considered themselves underprivileged!

Other social changes directly affecting the historical family unit structure included latchkey children and child-minding centers. These enabled both parents to keep earning the money required to provide the latest fad and fashion while simultaneously enabling their offspring to keep living in the expensive manner to which they had grown accustomed.

With so many changes to the family unit over the last ten to twenty years, and much well-meaning discussion regarding the breakdown of the family unit, it might be time to initiate something more substantial in an effort to identify a structure more suited to the twenty-first century. Perhaps that will be the role played by the experts involved in the family therapy field.

Treating the family as a whole unit rather than separate individuals is one uniform practice shared by most therapists.

The therapy is based on the belief that a troubled person should not be seen in isolation from the family unit. For example, a disturbed child may reflect parental conflicts rather than an underlying problem restricted to the child.

Family therapy is now at the stage where the information gleaned from many case histories can be used to determine the internal elements that make for a happy, cohesive family unit. It is no coincidence that the various elements are the same as those required for a happy, cohesive relationship of any kind.

Happy Families Share Routines and Dreams.

Unity of any kind is impossible without the give and take that flows from sharing responsibilities, chores, sympathies, or involvements. In such an atmosphere, it is possible to develop a dream and have it supported and nurtured through to its realization.

Happy Families do not Allow Conflict to Turn into an Ongoing Resentment.

Communication is the key to avoiding the downfall of so many relationships between two or more people. Any argument or dispute should be resolved within a short time span following the altercation, because most people sincerely wish for a speedy return to peaceful coexistence rather than a drawn-out saga inevitably resulting in **regret** or **guilt**. Actively seeking a way to cool down and heal any rift caused by heated words provides a far more mature and satisfying feeling than allowing the heat to simmer in silence and without apparent hope of a resolution and reconciliation.

Happy Families Learn to be Flexible in Their Thinking and Attitudes.

Flexible thinking and action allow others *"to be"* and are therefore vital components in any kind of relationship. They give others the opportunity to explore, to seek, to understand, to challenge, thus allowing the unrestricted release of talent and potential via a gift from the universe known as **freedom of expression.**

One of the dangers associated with a negative-styled "close family" is a tendency to become overprotective or overindulgent, effectively stifling freedom of expression along with all its exceptional benefits.

A manipulative, dominant head of the family creates a close family by using the expression, *"the family comes first"* as a means of controlling the lives of all family members. The main purpose of the exercise is to place a psychological anchor that conditions the family members to think twice about moving too far from the family environment.

Compare that situation with one where the head of the family develops closeness by practicing and encouraging openness in thought, word, deed, and action. In that kind of environment, the *"family comes first"* philosophy becomes unconditional, and members can obtain the freedom to pursue their desired independent identity.

Happy Families Feel at Home With Each Other.

Tolerance is an essential behavioral element in the development and sustaining of any relationship. The first step for achieving the highly desirable attribute of tolerance is to recognize and accept your personal imperfections. The second step is to set about correcting any imperfections you may have, considering them to be having a detrimental effect on your personal quality of life. The third and probably most important step is to acknowledge, accept, and be tolerant of other people's idiosyncrasies, foibles, and funny little habits.

Tolerance practiced by all members of a family creates a harmonious atmosphere that allows:

- *Routines and dreams to be shared*
- *Conflict to be kept to a minimum and controlled*
- *Flexible thinking to flourish*
- *Each family member to feel at home with each other*

There is an absence of any need or inclination for power or mind games. Respect for each other's privacy is observed, but as soon as the desire for personal space is sated, interactive contact

The 10-Year Glitch

and communication once again become the way of close-knit family life. When all the foregoing positive elements are the rule rather than the exception, then it is truly a case of there being, *"no place like home."*

CHAPTER SEVEN

The Highest Form of Expectation

Living up to other people's expectations rather than your own is one way of missing the point of having an earthly experience. Striving to be anything other than their individual selves is one of the major reasons for many people falling short of their own expectation. In trying to live up to the expectations set by parents, teachers, friends, partners, children, or religion, a person relinquishes the chance to explore stimulating, character-building elements of self-growth and development. Liberation from other people's opinions, criticism, or manipulation is, of course, one of the most important elements for virtually any aspect of the earthly experience, and it is certainly an essential prerequisite in the area of **expectation**.

The inability or unwillingness to break free from a dominating, constricting influence will prove a constant barrier to the attainment of worthwhile expectation rewards and achievements. Worthwhile expectations generally have, as their initial thrust:

The 10-Year Glitch

- *A wish*
- *A dream*
- *A desire*

Converting them into an expectation that delivers the anticipated result will greatly depend on how ardent the wish or grandiose the dream or burning the desire. Depending on how lofty or all encompassing the expectation, personal changes will invariably need to be made in areas such as:

- *Beliefs*
- *Attitude*
- *Behavior*
- *Performance*

All have a defining link with:

- *Ambition*
- *Achievement*
- *Anticipation*
- *Opportunity elements that are closely associated with expectations*

Opportunity is the most influential of the elements because it provides the opening that allows the expectation to start its process journey from wish, dream, or desire. Conversely, the perceived lack of opportunities will act as an insurmountable obstacle in the pursuit of expectations.

Very few other things in the universe are more abundant than opportunities. However, to gain the advantages offered

The Highest Form of Expectation

by opportunities in personal growth, intellectual development, financial security, or any other quality-of-life enhancement, the opportunity first has to be **recognized**. Secondly, some kind of **preparation** must enable the opportunity to be fully exploited.

Although opportunities are in plentiful supply for those seeking them out, there are also a number of reasons why opportunities can appear elusive and even non-existent. It is difficult to see or attract opportunities if one is too busy, too tired, too mentally lazy, too ensconced in an ambition-limiting comfort zone, too suspicious, too cautious, or **too influenced by other people's opinions**—the perennial psychological millstone!

Nothing undermines high expectations or any level of expectation for that matter, faster and more adversely than the external advice suggesting the opportunity someone is contemplating is perhaps beyond his/her capabilities and, therefore, not a realistic option.

What if I get it wrong? becomes the recurring question of life, covering the fear of making a mistake.

People in their early stages of spiritual awareness are prone to becoming victims of the *"good advice for your own sake"* type of unsolicited suggestion. In many instances, however, people ready and willing to offer opportunity-stifling advice often do not have ambition, aspirations, or expectations of their own. They are therefore incapable of seeing and recognizing an opportunity either for themselves or someone else!

Making mistakes provides one of the many ironies of life, as it is an integral component in self-development and will on occasion lead to unexpected rewards. So was it really a mistake, or was it simply a decision made when presented with more than one option, leaving the person with the resolve to try another option next time?

The 10-Year Glitch

Advice intended to stop someone from making a mistake is extremely poor advice, because expectations achieved through trial and error can produce results as satisfying as those achieved via the preparation process can. Every decision brings its own experience with it. In that light, it is never a mistake, simply an experience with its own consequences. As we reach maturity, we are the sum total of our experiences. This is recognized as our **character**.

The recurring question, *What if I get it wrong?* when associated with expectation, brings into play the other recurring question, *Should I fear the future?*

A fear of future expectation is a debilitating thought process that is just as destructive and energy sapping as having no expectations for the future. To be constantly fearful of perceived or imagined future problems, disasters, or impossible situations is to eliminate or otherwise destroy the sheer exhilaration available from living, loving, and sharing every present moment. To avoid or overcome the fear, it is perhaps a wise move to ignore messages and messengers promoting or dwelling on the negative, doom-laden aspects of past, present, and future.

The philosophy *"what you don't know can't hurt you"* is an ideal peace-of-mind affirmation for coping with and enjoying right here, right now. The opposite of the **future fearer** is the person who expects everything to remain as it was and is. That is a recipe for major disappointment whenever progress, or a new generation of thinking, or a dramatic shift in the status quo, challenges deep-rooted tradition. To expect things to remain the same is to defy the logic that states, *"What **was** ultimately must become what **is**."* That progress cycle has never varied from the beginning of time, and it never will.

In the parent-children relationship, expectations from both sides are severely challenged because parents are products of the past, children are products of the present, and both have their own, often opposite, idea of future expectations. A serious aspect of the expectation subject occurs when society creates a situation whereby expectations are removed or made extremely difficult to contemplate.

For many years, a worldwide expectation existed that was built upon a *"40-year plan."* Young adults completed their education, joined the work force, retired after forty years in a secure job or career, and received a pension as a reward for all the taxes they contributed during their working life. The promise of a job at the end of the education cycle provided the first expectation experience for young adults. In wondering why there is an increasing number of disillusioned and frustrated young people, society need look no further than the end of the 40-year plan and the failure to provide a workable substitute.

A by-product of expectation deficiency is the growth of a subculture made up of people expecting to have their every need and requirement supplied and catered to without necessarily contributing anything substantial in return. It is difficult and probably unfair to criticize, because many of them are the victims of a society that failed to see or acknowledge the repercussions of a shrinking job market and the virtual end of job security. To counteract the failing, various governments of the day spend millions of dollars creating **expectation mirages** with all kinds of apparent advantages linked to health, welfare, education, and job-creation schemes that look good from a distance but fade dramatically at the touch and feel stage.

In spiritual thinking and teaching, there seems to be answers for all that was, all that is, and all that will be. However, there is one vital element required in order to receive the full bonus available for being willing to think, reason, analyze, and accept ideas beyond the mainstream limitations.

The adage, *"actions speak louder than words"* sits admirably when applied to the pursuit of any kind or type of expectation.

The 10-Year Glitch

Without doubt, achieving a desired expectation result requires effort, backed up by varying degrees of patience, persistence, and determination, all of which thrive on action as their source of inspiration and motivation.

Roman philosopher and spiritual leader Publius Syrus supplied a poignant reminder of human potential with his observation *"No one knows what they can do until they try."* In addition, without doubt, those who want but refuse to act will want all their lives.

Family health (or ill health) is one area of expectation requiring vigilant awareness during each of the 10-Year Glitch cycles. Many people constantly dwell on hereditary disease or health conditions with oft-repeated statements such as *"Weak hearts run in the family, so I guess I'll suffer from it when I'm older."* This is a powerful affirmation capable of ultimately creating the complaint in what could have been an otherwise healthy body destined for healthy longevity!

Another misplaced and highly damaging affirmation occurs with the oft-repeated expression *"I'm a battler, and I'll always be a battler, because nothing good ever happens in my life."* Unfortunately, that mindset becomes expectation, which will often result in the **sabotage** of anything good happening, followed by the utterance, *"There, I told you so."*

Some outcomes in life can exceed expectations, thus presenting a decision either to be satisfied with the better-than-anticipated achievement or to aim for an even higher level of achievement. One or other of the recurring questions of life will certainly play a role in the decision making.

Conversely, it is possible to be carried away with an expectation and to have it crash down when it falls short of the mark. It can happen when too much is left to chance or fate rather than personal effort and preparation.

The Highest Form of Expectation

"When you pray, you have to move your feet" is an expression that sums up the danger of relying on too much external influence for achieving an expectation.

Can I start again? will be the recurring question of life, requiring serious appraisal following any expectation disaster.

The starting point of the path leading to the realization of great expectations is the decision to live one's life according to self-imposed standards, beliefs, and values. Because they are self-imposed, they need have no limitations in size or scope.

The universe has provided an element called **perfection** that allows unlimited scope for achieving expectations of almost any magnitude. The very pursuit of perfection can lift any human far above the average or ordinary. The true value of perfection is not in the attainment of it, a rare feat, but in the striving to attain it via the use of imagination and visualization to picture the perfect result.

Once the picture of perfection is firmly lodged in the mind, the physical pursuit becomes elevated to the realms of **inspiration**. The universe is filled with examples of finished products derived from the process.

When inspiration is added to any state of mind, every endeavor flowing from the combination is immediately elevated to a level best described as the highest form of expectation. At this level, the impossible is made possible, dreams become reality, and achievement becomes a foregone conclusion.

The 10-Year Glitch

Chapter Eight

A Lesson in Learning

"*Why is this happening again?*" is a question many people will ask at some time during the earthly experience. Utter frustration is usually the cause for the need to ask the question, with the frustration triggered by things not going according to personal plans. A vital element requiring inclusion in any analysis of the question is the acceptance that the earthly experience is a non-stop **lesson-in-learning journey** from arrival to departure.

A variety of lessons is presented throughout each one of the seven decades. One way to avoid a 10-Year Glitch is to deal with the lessons as they occur. In pre-teen years, the lesson object is to learn how to walk, talk, and live life according to the direction and teaching of parents. In teenage years, a process called **seeking independence** means the lesson object now is to learn how to start living life according to the teachings of anyone other than parents! Immediately beyond the teenage years, the real lessons of life begin.

Life itself is the great teacher, but unfortunately, the classroom is not always filled with attentive, interested pupils. However, like it or not, life will keep hammering the lessons repeatedly until inattention or disinterest is replaced by awareness and acceptance. For some pupils, awareness and acceptance take a considerable slice of a lifetime, punctuated by an oft-repeated cry of, *"Why does this **keep** happening to me?"*

There are many theories offered up on the subject of learning, but no single theory can account for the complexities involved in the process. Traditional medical theories regarding learning involve two main elements: behavioral patterns that emphasize the role of conditioning in learning and a concept that learning occurs through the building of abstract **cognitive models,** using mental capacities, such as:

- *Intelligence*
- *Memory*
- *Insight*
- *Understanding*

Social learning theories combine aspects of both behavioral and cognitive learning theories, and it is probable some things are learned by conditioning and others by complex thought processes that take account of many facts.

Learning difficulties, as expounded by traditional medical practitioners, stem from a range of psychological and physical problems that interfere with learning. Difficulties may be either general or specific. Examples of specific learning difficulties include:

- *Dyslexia* (difficulty in reading or word blindness)
- *Dyscalculia* (inability to solve mathematical problems)
- *Dysgraphia* (writing disorders)

A Lesson in Learning

In most cases, the cause of a specific learning disability cannot be ascertained. Some psychologists now believe forms of minimal brain dysfunction, possibly genetic, may cause specific learning difficulties in children of normal intelligence. Although hearing and vision problems are treated as learning difficulties, emotional or environmental deprivations are generally not classified as learning difficulties.

The latest round of discussion on the subject of learning is centered on the increasing incidence of Attention Deficit Disorder, or A.D.D., and Attention Deficit Hyperactivity Disorder, or A.D.H.D. The major problem with converting theory into practical solutions is that A.D.D. and A.D.H.D. are, or can be, a *combination* of specific emotional, environmental, and dietary conditions. As with many traditional medical theories, there is often an elusive quality preventing a black-and-white explanation. So it is with the subject of learning.

The dietary aspect of A.D.H.D. was demonstrated to us some years ago when a client's son, who was about ten years old at the time, was being chastised at school and labeled as disruptive in class. He was also very cruel to his younger sister at home and generally badly behaved. His mother discussed the situation during one of her counseling sessions and was naturally concerned about the boy's behavior.

We suggested she consult a kinesiologist in a nearby town who placed a lot of emphasis on allergies and the effect on behavioral problems. Kinesiology balances health by testing muscles and ascertaining through this practice the sensitivity or allergic reaction to some foods. Practitioners believe that each group of muscles is related to other parts of the body, such as the organs, digestive system, glands, bones, and circulation. How a muscle responds in tests reveals how the whole body is functioning.

The 10-Year Glitch

The practitioner eliminated many known allergens from the boy's diet such as yeast, dairy products, wheat, artificial colorings, and preservatives. Although the boy was less than pleased with his limited diet, he and his mother did persevere. Within a few weeks, his behavior improved and continued to do so until he was a pleasant, well-behaved, cooperative child. Certain foods could gradually be reintroduced in the ensuing months, but several stayed on the forbidden list. The belief that a healthy child is a happy, well-adjusted child also proved that, conversely, an unhealthy child is more likely to develop behavioral problems, including A.D.D and A.D.H.D.

It is said that you cannot accomplish anything with just theory, which explains why life, when in teaching mode, adds great chunks of practicality to any lessons handed out. The lessons are not always palatable, welcome, or indeed understood (at the time). Nevertheless, they have to be endured in order to obtain the eventual reward for absorbing the lessons and learning from them!

As stated earlier, life is the great teacher—life sets the earthly experience curriculum, with many of the lesson subjects being set via the recurring questions of life. One of life's more favored ways of teaching a lesson is also one of the most feared—*learning from mistakes.* It would not be the preferred choice of most people, yet it is perhaps the most stimulating, rewarding, and satisfying way to achieve ultimate success, correct a negative situation, or answer the question, *"Why is this happening again?"*

The German poet and dramatist Goethe supplied the world with a great wisdom when he said, *"It is possible that all mistakes lead to an inestimable gain."* Learning from mistakes enables people to gain **experience**, the most valuable of all earthly personal growth possessions. The expression *"learning from experience"* is a subtle reminder to avoid making the same mistake or decision when faced with the same situation more than once. The inability to supply a positive answer to the recurring question of life, *Should I fear the future?* is usually the result of regularly making the same decision even when it has been found that the decision was unpalatable.

Logically, if one keeps doing the same thing, one will attain the same result.

Is there a common character trait shared by mistake-prone people? Perhaps the most common and obvious traits are:

- *Too stubborn*
- *Too conceited*
- *Too arrogant*
- *Too lazy to learn*

A mind too often affected by stimulant-type drugs is a fairly new but fast-growing reason for an existence embattled by poor decision making. Being too eager to please, or too available to satisfy other people's needs, is also a formula for this repetition.

The recurring question of life:

- *What if I get it wrong?* provides the challenge for all decisions stemming from two other recurring questions, both of which involve the specter of making a mistake.
- *When should I say it is over?*
- *Can I start again?*

An element closely associated with these three recurring questions is the element of risk. To understand the relationship between mistakes, experience, and risk is to understand the learning experience as it applies to daily life.

There are three main risk factors:

- *Calculated*
- *Wishful*
- *Reckless*

The very moment a person decides on a course of action with an element of risk involved, one of the three risk factors will accompany the decision. Before exploring that outcome, it is essential to study what happens when people faced with one of the three recurring questions decide not to make a decision for fear of making a wrong decision.

What if I get it wrong? What if you do?

History has innumerable examples demonstrating how the most valuable lessons of life have come as a direct result of a risk taken, a mistake made, a life-enhancing experience gained. The major reward for taking a risk is the gaining of a personal growth education that simply cannot be obtained by any other means.

Learning something about self is a valuable by-product of deciding to take a risk to overcome, eliminate, improve, change, or correct an unsatisfactory situation, especially when the recurring question, *When should I say it is over?* is demanding a courageous and instant answer.

Although risk taking is generally associated with financial affairs, it is in the area of relationships that fear of making a wrong decision can do so much damage to individuals. What is a wrong decision when applied to a relationship? If a couple discovers after a number of years that they are wrong for each other, must they stay together and continue the mistake? Should they now be extra wary of making the same decision again? It really does not matter how the questions are answered, because the recurring question, *When should I say it is over?* Will ultimately provide the deciding factor one way or another.

In seeking a clear, uncomplicated answer to the question, it is well to know that external advice, such as *"Are you sure you're not making a mistake?"* will muddy and complicate the decision-making process by casting a shadow of doubt. The fact is, no matter how concerned or caring the person posing the question, personal growth of any substance is best obtained by making personal decisions and surviving the consequences.

"Live and learn" is possibly as good as any other philosophy for traveling life's journey. Learning to recognize the difference between the calculated, wishful, and reckless risk will greatly increase the comfort of the trip. As suggested previously, all three can sometimes be involved at various stages during a major decision-making time.

The calculated risk relies very much on previous experience to be considered reliable. If decision makers do not have the necessary experience, they will often rely on someone that does have the experience. Therein dwells a hidden risk that could turn out later to be wishful or even reckless if things go terribly wrong.

The wishful risk is generally emotion charged, relying extensively on what is ardently desired, regardless of any logical consideration. It often succeeds because the motivation of desire, coupled with logic-free determination, is an irresistible force capable of overcoming mistake-centered obstacles. Other people's opinions or advice rarely become involved, which is possibly the reason for its high rate of success.

Although *the reckless risk* is not for the faint-hearted, it is one enabling giant steps to be taken in fields of human endeavor where challenging the unknown and overcoming the seemingly impossible would not have been achieved in any other way.

Regardless of the risk, poor decision, or lesson, the thing that really counts is willingness to learn. Academic learning has a particular role to play, but it will remain a partial role compared to the learning required for spiritual growth and development.

It is from that development that the human race learns to:

- *Love*
- *Forgive*
- *Tolerate*
- *Share*
- *Shoulder*
- *Exchange*
- *Preserve*
- *Exist*
- *Care*
- *Heal*
- *Give*
- *Offer*
- *Appreciate*
- *Bless*

Spiritual development will provide the teachers able to demonstrate the kind of leadership that does not rely

A Lesson in Learning

on military might, money, violence, laws, or political manipulations. So many lessons, so much to learn, so vital to acknowledge and accept unconditionally.

Learn every lesson well this time around!

The 10-Year Glitch

CHAPTER NINE

It is a Long Road That Has No Signposts

Life's great journey can be either a long, arduous slog or a reasonably comfortable ride, given the odd bump or two along the way. The element often making the difference is the appreciation of an extremely important aspect of life called the **crossroad sign factor**.

Every traveler, on a regular basis, will be required to confront this factor voluntarily. On some occasions, it will be thrust upon him or her by way of a mini or major crisis.

On any very long journey, a crossroad signpost is often a welcome relief. It gives essential and accurate directions and provides the comfort of knowing you are exactly where you should be at that point. If you are going in the wrong direction, or lost, the signpost acts as a guide by indicating the way to return to your originally intended route.

The crossroad signpost is especially welcome if the journey thus far has been on a long road that had no turning. Nowadays, of course, that same road would have a fast food outlet every few miles!

Reaching crossroads in one's life can also provide welcome relief because it offers the chance to pause for a while, allowing time to check on the recurring question, *Am I where I should be?*

Aiding and abetting the answering process is the aspect of life that plays a leading role in virtually all decision making—quality of thought. According to scientific research data, the average human mind receives thousands of thoughts per day. Naturally, the majority of those thoughts are not in the earth-shattering class. They are more the fleeting type of thought requiring minimum mind space due to their inconsequential nature.

The second category of thoughts are those associated with the current day's activities and can include what to eat, what to wear, where to go, what to do, who to see, and who to avoid. Most of these thoughts are habit forming and therefore easily absorbed into a daily routine with little fuss or bother.

It is the third category of thought that brings the crossroad signpost factor into sharp focus. Regardless of the length of any particular life span, it is sure to be interrupted every now and then by the need to face some kind of crisis. To overcome the distraction caused by the crisis, a decision has to be made that may alter the direction in which life was moving before the arrival of the crisis.

A major crisis often means a drastic decision, resulting in a more dramatic change in direction. A number of recurring questions of life will invariably need to be faced in the aftermath of the crisis.

- *Am I where I should be?*
- *Can I start again?*
- *Should I fear the future?*

Again, regardless of the severity or nature of the crisis, it will take courage to face and accept the crisis and then make a resolving type of decision, enabling life to return quickly to reasonably orderly progress. Failing to make a decision of some kind will often lead to the crisis increasing its influence to the point where crisis becomes catastrophe! At that point, the crossroad decision option is withdrawn from those personally involved and given to an outside source to provide a resolution.

In some instances, the need for a crossroad decision can start to become obvious long before it actually arrives. Many crisis incidents gather strength from a series of seemingly insignificant events that are either not recognized as having sinister long-term implications or, if recognized, are ignored as not being as bad as they seem. Unfortunately, in life's journey, that attitude can be likened to taking a detour. Inevitably, the detour returns the traveler to the original route.

The warning signs of impending trouble can include:

- *Relying on others to make your decisions, or always seeking advice before making a decision*

- *Failing to deal with minor irritations that eventually become major distractions*

- *Repeatedly asking, "Why is this happening again?" after realizing that the things going wrong are outnumbering the things going right*

- *Procrastinating over financial, social, or health decisions to the point where procrastination becomes as pronounced as any other daily habit*

- *Constantly thinking about a change in career, social circle, environment, or relationship, but avoiding the issue each time the crossroad signpost looms up before you*

Appreciating that **thoughts are things** is the first step in recognizing the early warning signs. It is also arguably one of the most important life skills necessary to first survive, and secondly enjoy, the earthly experience. The thought process simply cannot be taken too lightly.

Every move, every act, every cause, every effect experienced, is motivated, regulated, and often manipulated by either a single thought or a series of thoughts.

Thoughts are to the Mind What Cells are to the Body.

Positive, vibrant, non-limiting thoughts help to keep the mind healthy in a manner similar to how the physical body is kept healthy by cells enriched with sufficient and balanced amounts of vitamins and minerals.

Good-quality Thoughts act as Nutrients for the Mind.

Regardless of how big or small, it must be realized that thoughts are also highly elusive. They flit across the vast space of the universe, available to all, but the property of none, until attracted to the mind willing and able to receive the embryo and convert its destination into destiny.

"One day I will...," the oft-repeated phrase of the procrastinator, only remains in thought form for a limited time. If dreams, ambitions, or goals are not turned into a physical reality, the thought is released back into the ether to be received by another mind in another place.

Life's great journey has many stragglers. They are the commuters who spurn the crossroad signpost factor that clearly pointed the way to a new and challenging direction. Their indecisiveness about whether to accept the sign leads to being stuck in a rut. In addition, persistent attempts to bypass obvious signs lead to a regular visit to cul-de-sacs.

The spiritual path is an interesting diversion away from the mainstream flow of life's great journey. Many fail to negotiate this route when first confronted with the need to take an alternative direction. Sadly, and yet almost divinely, it is often the case that a major crisis triggers the impetus for the beginning of the spiritual journey—a journey providing the serenity of thought and peace of mind so essential for offsetting any pain, hardship, or heartache caused by the crisis.

Being truly comfortable while striding purposefully along the spiritual path often leads to the discovery of exciting new positive values and attitudes. The trinkets and baubles of mainstream life, often considered so important and essential, are seen from a new, mature, and enlightened perspective. They seem almost petty in comparison to the clarity of thought and clearness of vision the spiritual path affords all those with open, receptive minds.

One destructive state of mind, capable of hindering the ability to accept any kind of crossroad signpost direction, is known as **self-limiting** thoughts. They supply all the reasons for not accepting any deviation from a well-trodden path. In turn, life's great journey is changed from a relatively smooth-surfaced experience to one pitted with potholes, along with the occasional crater. Life, it seems, demands that if you think you **cannot** more often than you think you **can**, then any endeavor where success of some kind is desired will prove a frustratingly elusive exercise.

One method of preparing for the arrival of a crossroad signpost decision is to acknowledge that the journey through life can never be completely trouble-free or problem-free. This is due to the necessity for learning one of life's essential lessons: *Character building and development.*

Nowadays, the building and development of character is included in the all-encompassing field of personal growth. One vital element in the process of character building, and any of the other personal growth areas, is the control and eventual elimination of the aforementioned self-limiting thoughts. These stifle potential, dash dreams, counteract ambition, and are the foundation upon which *indecision* is built. Anyone who has experienced the excitement caused by a great idea and a subsequent disappointment as the exhilaration waned will probably have fallen victim to the self-limiting thought process.

The big idea, grand plan, uplifting dream, and burning ambition, are all pure, unaffected thoughts when first received. If allowed to gather strength through mixing with energizing thoughts such as faith, persistence, and determination, it is almost guaranteed that the idea, plan, dream, or ambition will become a physical reality.

Thoughts received are only as good as the company they keep.

Therefore, when the pure, unaffected thoughts are exposed to negative, self-limiting thoughts, the chance for a successful outcome is greatly diminished—hence, the reason for the plunge from high expectation to low frustration.

Character and courage form an irresistible bond.

Life's great adventure, regardless of which road is being traveled at any particular time, will provide a regular test of character. Reaching a crossroad signpost decision time invariably presents the test of character and courage required in order to follow the signpost direction and comply with the sound, positive advice that states, *"The biggest and most courageous step on the road to fulfillment is the first step."*

It Is A Long Road That Has No Signposts

The inevitable outcome of not taking the first bold step when the crossroad signpost is clear and compatible with desired intentions is falling victim to an insidious mind aberration called regret. At the very core of most regrets is the feeling that something could and should have been done when the chance and opportunity existed.

The final correlation factor illustrating a character-courage link is contained in the perennial truth that states, *"Character is destiny."* It is, of course, difficult to accept a crossroad signpost direction to go forward if there are unresolved issues littering the journey just traveled.

If the past holds no ties, however, the crossroad signpost decision to continue the journey toward the life you want and deserve will be so much more rewarding, regardless of how long the journey may be.

The 10-Year Glitch

CHAPTER TEN

The Elusive Desire Called Freedom

"The day I stopped worrying about what people thought of me was the day I felt liberated as a human being."

Although the author of the above observation is unknown, the absolute wisdom of its philosophy is one of the best examples of how anyone can obtain a rewarding form of personal freedom. Freedom, in its variety of forms, is a highly desired condition of the life experience, but it is also one of the most elusive qualities to achieve.

As with so many other aspects of life, the desire to achieve a particular life experience must start with **self-motivation**. Therefore, a desire for freedom of thought, word, deed, expression, or choice cannot be obtained if self is a prisoner of other people's opinions, wishes, criticisms, or manipulations. Living a life afraid of what other people think can never lead to a good quality of life. To overcome this freedom-stifling situation, it is necessary to live life according to personal standards and beliefs so that they eventually become the values lived by rather than the values other people attempt to impose.

A good example of personal freedom is that which is lived by a **lost tribe**. A loss of personal freedom occurs when missionaries discover the lost tribe and decide to liberate them from their undesirable primitive existence.

One such example occurred not so long ago when a lost tribe was discovered in the rainforest of the Andaman Islands in the Bay of Bengal. The 400-strong Jarawasi tribe had survived for thousands of years in harmonious freedom, managing with ease and contentment to obtain from their surroundings the three essentials of life: food, clothing, and shelter.

Enter the meddlesome missionaries, who immediately enslaved the tribe with an all-encompassing freedom-destroyer known as religious dogma. The tribe was encouraged to give up its traditional lifestyles and merge with the rest of the outside world population.

Indian government officials were ultimately criticized for persuading the tribe to change its diet from wild fruits, nuts, and smoked meats to curries, sandwiches, and processed food. The change, along with other assimilation processes, led to the tribe contracting diseases unknown to their medicine men and healers.

This story is a perfect example of how any society, be it democratic, autocratic, or military-ruled, is far more comfortable when personal freedom of its citizens is restricted to a manageable and controlled level. Total freedom, of course, is unacceptable, because it can lead to a total disregard for all laws and authority directives, causing a condition known as anarchy.

However, there is a vast difference between disparate ruling bodies in dealing with freedom-restricting practices. Autocratic and military-ruled regimes enforce the restrictions openly and

The Elusive Desire Called Freedom

ruthlessly with the aid of secret police, guns, and brutality when required.

Democratic regimes achieve the same result but in a more subtle, underhanded way via a multitude of government departments, committees, and sub-committees, all enforcing freedom-restricting and controlling laws, rules, and red tape-bound regulations. Computer cross-referencing, with its unlimited potential for maintaining an acceptable level of control by the democratic leadership, is today's lethal freedom-restricting weapon.

The best way to take unwanted attention away from an unpalatable situation is to create a diversion. Democratic societies around the world have achieved this by developing lottery-type methods of gambling. The millions of dollars in prize money promising **financial freedom** is a perfect camouflage for the many covert, freedom-restricting operations.

The promise is a good example of **freedom illusion**, a condition providing short-term gratification. After receiving the lottery-winning check for a few million dollars, the recipient begins to enjoy life-long financial freedom—right up to the time when the tax-free lottery win becomes a taxable financial investment. Financial advisors are then needed to begin a continuous round of rolling the money over, under, sideways, and backwards in an expensive but ultimately futile attempt to minimize taxable income, resulting in the lottery winner lamenting about the **price of freedom**! It would be nice to think that one day soon the Jarawasi tribe will win the lottery, buy a remote island, become a lost tribe again, and preserve their freedom by surrounding the island with a missionary-proof fence!

A number of other freedom illusions are capable of providing short-term gratification. Most are harmless and merely supply a temporary release from some form of everyday living shackle. *"Getting away from it all"* or *"escaping from the rat race for a few weeks,"* along with the more permanent *"sea change,"* are popular expressions indicating people's constant need for freedom, no matter how fleeting.

A more sinister aspect of freedom illusion is the use and abuse of substances taken for the express purpose of obtaining an instant freedom-invoking feeling. Ultimately, substance use for that purpose simply **enslaves**!

According to current society speak, living in some countries means living in a free country, but what does that actually mean? There are many bounds within which the citizens of those countries must conduct their daily lives, as dictated by numerous laws of the land. Some consider those laws as restrictions on their personal freedom, while others say there should be more laws to cover particular areas where no laws exist at present.

One argument offered on the subject of freedom is that, in its purest sense, it is a state of mind. Therefore, as with so many other aspects of life, freedom starts with personal choice rather than the influence of others.

However, people can also see freedom differently. What one person perceives as freedom, another may see as a restriction. For example, some people, on hearing the suggestion, *"You are **free** to make your own decision,"* would feel extremely nervous and probably fearful of being offered a personal freedom choice. They would be anxious about not answering successfully the recurring question of life, *What if I get it wrong?*

Conversely, when a person is ready to accept the responsibility of making decisions based on his/her own analysis and judgment, he/she becomes empowered and capable of taking charge of his/her life, thus experiencing a special type of freedom. The philosopher Epictetus expressed the sentiment this way: *"No man is free who is not master of himself."*

The Elusive Desire Called Freedom

There are two definite ways to obtain a secure and permanent personal freedom. The first, while perhaps not most people's choice, is nevertheless a legitimate freedom, especially from other people's adverse influences. Eccentricity is possibly the purest, and certainly most honest, form of self-expression. The genuine eccentric has managed to break through barriers normally barring the way of any person desiring to free up his/her life from the constraints of conventional existence.

The few (too few) genuine eccentrics, both past and present, have often been ridiculed by people who are desperately striving to achieve the very thing the eccentric person has achieved—the ability to supply a resounding yes to the recurring question of life, *Am I who I want to be?*

In not caring what others think of their eccentric outlet, style of dress, manner of speech, or mode of conduct, eccentric people are not being selfish, although others often level this accusation at them. The people who insist the eccentric person should act in a more normal way are being selfish. They want the eccentric to conform, but the eccentric asks no more than to be allowed unconditional freedom of expression.

History shows that the true eccentric is a pioneer in the area of freedom thinking, and through that thinking, much of what now exists in the world was created, discovered, or came into being. Some eccentrics have, of course, been judged to have gone too far beyond normal, but any thinking capable of stretching beyond the boundaries considered normal will be condemned by those unable or unwilling to rid themselves of the fear of what others might think.

People who do not conform to the norm in their thinking or attitude are often accused of being unreasonable, or stubborn, or any other derogatory name, in an effort to change them to a more reasonable disposition. To truly answer the recurring question, *Am I who I want to be?* It does seem that some mild form of eccentric behavior is required in order to overcome other people's ideas of who they think you should be.

The second way of achieving personal freedom is certainly less adventuresome than eccentricity, but it will still require a similar kind of doggedness to hang onto thoughts, feelings, beliefs, and wisdoms, all of which detractors will label as not normal. It takes a measure of courage to allow the mind to reach out beyond normal in order to **explore**, **expand**, and **question**. When the decision is made to begin the search for personal freedom from earthbound roots, a remarkable mind function is available to assist with the enormous scope of the project.

The second way combines **spiritual awareness** and **imagination.** This combination is a perfect ally for those beginning the journey in search of their spiritual selves, as well as those who have arrived well and truly.

It is said that imagination is more important than knowledge, which can be interpreted to mean that knowledge is an earthbound attribute and therefore limited, whereas imagination is ethereal and therefore limitless. Because the bulk of spiritual beliefs are ethereal by nature, pursuit of them must inevitably mean abandoning the restrictions of earthbound knowledge. Also inevitably, it will mean alienating any person not of the same thinking or inclination. This is usually the first obstacle for awakening spiritual seekers to overcome, and often the opposition comes from relatives or friends.

In the face of opposition, it is important to remember that imagination, if kept private and personal, cannot be adversely influenced by an outside source. It provides freedom and liberation from other people's opinions, criticisms, or manipulations and is so powerful that it can change even the most vitriolic opposition.

The Elusive Desire Called Freedom

It is rare for any person discovering, using, and enjoying the spiritual experience to be swayed away from and returned to the normal or reasonable earthbound, freedom-restricting way of thinking, because he/she is as close as anyone is to experiencing the elusive desire called freedom.

The 10-Year Glitch

CHAPTER ELEVEN

Magic is Not All Illusion

Do you believe in magic?
Do you believe in miracles?
Do you believe in a higher power?

Whether you believe in one, two, or all three, you may have already experienced some amazing events in your life because the three are irresistibly entwined. The purest meaning of magic states, *"The art of influencing events by occult control of nature and spirits,"* with black and white magic identified as malevolent (black) and benevolent (white). The expression, *"Life is not all black or white,"* suggests that many grey areas exist merely to indulge life's kind and cruel **twists of fate**.

When the word **magic** is used in day-to-day life, the meaning is more toward the benevolent side and usually heralds the happening of a special moment, event, or occasion. A by-product of this is known as good luck. Bad luck is the day-to-day connection for the darker side of the magic equation. Good and bad luck, along with happenings considered magic moments, all have as their core source of energy the powerful force called ***the law of attraction***.

Like many universal laws, it is a demanding law not disposed toward emotionally distinguishing between good and bad. It simply reacts on the direction given to it by **thoughts**. Positive thoughts will attract good luck and magic moments while simultaneously repelling elements of a detrimental nature. Conversely, negative thoughts will attract bad luck while simultaneously repelling magic moments.

Magic moments are not generally coincidental, nor are they freely available to unreceptive minds such as those described as closed, inflexible, negative, or pessimistic. In fact, those types of minds repel, ward off, and even reject situations that could have led to a magic moment. Even worse, negative minds can stop people close to them from attracting the opportunity of a magic moment experience.

Magic moments, along with the occasional miracle, will be attracted to minds regarded as open, curious, questioning, flexible, positive, optimistic, and spiritually aware. Those types of minds attract forces, people, and life elements able to supply the harmonious components of magic moments, good luck, and minor miracles.

Money, a powerful energy source, is also highly sensitive to the universal **law of attraction** and is a leading player in both magic moments and good or bad luck.

- *A money-conscious state of mind will attract the forces, people, and life elements necessary for an adequate supply of money energy.*
- *A poverty-conscious state of mind will repel these forces, people, and life elements, resulting in an inadequate supply of money energy.*

It would be naïve to ignore the influence money exerts in virtually all earthbound activities and experiences. When used for the right and honorable reason and purpose, money is an energy source powerful enough to attract all manner of magic moments. The late Mother Teresa's seemingly miracle-like humanitarian work was assisted by generous financial donations from her many admirers.

When money is used without the good of mankind as its motivation, it can become *"the root of all evil,"* often releasing the malevolent elements that undermine society's foundation and structure. Gambling is perhaps the most potent example of a life experience capable of shifting from white to grey to black in a very short space of time.

Can Magic Moments be Created or Orchestrated?

The answer is yes, as far as the gambling industry is concerned, and it spends millions of dollars promoting that kind of message. As a purely self-controlled social outlet, gambling can and does provide magic moments for people enjoying the occasional flutter. However, the good or bad, constructive or destructive, element arises and is determined by how far the gambler is prepared to tempt chance.

Money presents a continuous and often severe test of character inasmuch as it is associated with more positive and negative character traits than any other aspect of life. People and money exist in a paradoxical relationship, covering areas such as spending, saving, worshipping, despising, hoarding, circulating, revering, and resenting.

Whatever one's attitude toward the subject of money, it is worth noting the thought expressed by French philosopher Albert Camus, who said, *"It is a kind of spiritual snobbery that makes people think they can be happy without money."*

Another aspect of magic moments worth exploring is their therapeutic value when past magic moments are remembered in order to provide inspiration or comfort in the present. Special moments, incidents, and pleasant occasions from the past can prove a rich source of meditation material able to promote an instant stress-reducing exercise. Whenever the mind, body, or both begin tensing from some form of duress, recall a pleasing, wholly satisfying memory of a truly magic moment and hold it until the mind or body return to a stress-free condition.

Remember…the physical state cannot react to two thoughts at the same time.

It takes only moments to achieve a satisfying result. With practice, the mind will go into recall mode without a great deal of coercion. The magic moment recall method is also an excellent cure for insomnia. The inability to fall asleep is often caused by the mind being full of thoughts about today's or tomorrow's events and happenings. Recalling a tranquil, passive occasion that occurred in idyllic, picturesque surroundings will ultimately soothe away annoying, sleep-depriving thoughts.

A curious, questioning mind will lead its owner into many magic moments during a life span. A mind with those attributes will probe and search for ever more knowledge and, in some instances, investigate beyond what is currently known and accepted.

The great inventors Edison, Marconi, and Morse all created **miracles** during their lives in the fields of light, sound, vision, and communication. Definitions of miracle include: *Event due to supernatural agency; act of supernatural power; remarkable event; wonderful specimen of some quality.*

The latter two definitions enable the essence of miracle to be used freely for things in the earthbound existence, such as the Internet's World Wide Web and the computer age in general.

A first-prize lottery win against odds of 55 million to 1 qualifies as a miracle. A major accident or disaster where everyone survives is usually summed up by the expression *"It's a miracle no one was killed."*

For many adults, the ability they had as children to recognize and enjoy magic moments is no longer part of their psyche. A child's ability to be rendered **spellbound** demonstrates the use of imagination and the suspension of credibility for a limited time. Retaining the sense of wonderment is a good way adults can increase their chances of attracting a steady supply of magic moments. If the sense-of-wonderment ability has been lost, spending less thought time and emphasis on how busy, stressed, or impossible life is and more time devoted to wholehearted escapism can go a long way toward recapturing the life-enhancing quality. To miss the magic of the moment continually is to be a victim of a society enamored with and engrossed in unimaginative, self-centered activity.

There is one piece of magic freely available to all, but it is not used often enough considering the pleasure it gives to both giver and receiver. Behavioral therapists suggest that a genuine smile can help to make nine out of ten people respond favorably toward you within seconds of meeting them. Furthermore, they will usually return the smile, thus ensuring a pleasant meeting regardless of the purpose for the meeting.

The magic of a smile has long been used to thaw the frostiest disposition. It is also the first "manipulative" skill a baby uses to captivate doting adults. Like the baby's smile, the adult smile must come from deep within and give pleasure to both themselves and the receivers of the smile.

But what about that tenth person…the one that does not respond to the smile?

Perhaps they are the victims of a society hell-bent on promoting and selling expensive, gimmick-ridden, orchestrated magic moments. Their failure to smile could indicate a life so far devoid of genuine magic moments, because a life is unfulfilled if it is not built upon a foundation of many magic moments.

The most important thing is to make sure that tenth person is not you!

Chapter Twelve

You Are Only as Old as Your Age

Humans record their earthly experience in the most logical, mathematically correct, and orderly fashion by way of birthdays. Unfortunately, rather than allow the perfect process to proceed in the logical, mathematically correct, orderly fashion from conception to conclusion, humans are more attuned to taking something apart to see why it is in perfect working order.

The natural consequence of such action is that whatever nature created and offered as a perfect specimen ends up as a mongrel version of its original, pure self. Many of the world's sensitive environmental areas are good examples of this heavy-handed treatment. Although the result is the cause for much bewilderment and consternation, the treatment pales when compared to humans' treatment of age!

A few oft-used, age-connected expressions provide an insightful view of the confusing messages that result from converting the perfect to the imperfect.

The 10-Year Glitch

1. "At your age, you should know better."
2. "Don't be so childish."
3. "You're not old enough to be doing that."
4. "You're too old to be doing that."
5. "Why don't you grow up?"
6. "You don't look your age."
7. "You look good for your age."

Starting from early years, humans spend most of their earthly experience in conflict with their true age. At some time or another, they will deny, change, embellish it, wish to be older by adding a year or two, or wish to be younger by subtracting a year or two. They celebrate the twenty-first birthday and dread the fortieth. For many, the whole process starts in childhood in a seemingly harmless pursuit known as dress-up.

However, it is far from being an innocuous game played by innocents—it is rather the initial thrust for a lifetime of **age subterfuge**. In wearing their parents' clothes and accessories and mimicking their mannerisms, children become pretend adults, thus sowing the seed for a future where age-pretense becomes a way of life. For the child, the enjoyment of dress-up is short-lived and quickly curtailed with the onset of dreaded age-confusing instructions, such as:

- *"You're too young."*
- *"You can do that when you grow up."*
- *"When you're my age, you'll understand."*
- *"I wasn't allowed to do half the things you're allowed to do when I was your age."*

The yearning for age expression gathers serious momentum in the teenage years. The dress-up stage is the major casualty. Teenagers are horrified at the thought of wearing clothes or accessories their parents favored, opting instead for clothes and accessories their parents would be horrified at the thought of wearing.

The teenage years are the beginning of rules and regulations aimed at restricting age manipulation. Unfortunately, that is a recipe for direct conflict between those setting the rules and regulations and the teenagers, who specialize in a particular age manipulation known as **age advancement.** This is considered an essential life skill created for the sole purpose of enabling underage teenagers to participate in adult pursuits. Teenage efforts to disregard the rules and regulations blatantly are condemned by all manner of society watchdogs, most of who conveniently forget their own blatant disregard of the same rules and regulations during their own teenage years!

For an ever-increasing number of people, age deception gathers pace not long after the first bloom of youth starts to fade. The fading of the bloom heralds the immediate beginning of the thought-provoking, mystifying, and occasionally terrifying element known as ***the aging process.*** Without a doubt, this is the time in life when the truism *"It's all in the mind"* takes on a significant importance. The aging process is obviously a major mind-involving exercise for the majority of people during one or more of the decades.

It is true to say our way of life and circumstances clearly affect the speed of the aging process. However, an increasing and varied number of experts now subscribe to the theory that how a person thinks plays a vital role in the pace and quality of the aging process.

- *For some, it is the fear of aging.*
- *For others, it is the curse of aging.*
- *For a few, it is the "gentle contentment" of aging.*

The latter are the people who have accepted and conditioned their minds to the following philosophy: you are only as old as your age; you will only ever be as old as your age; and all the subterfuge, manipulation, and wishful thinking imaginable will not alter, change, or reverse the situation.

Before exploring the weird, wonderful, daring, puzzling, and often outrageous ways people try to prove the philosophy wrong by attempting to cheat the aging process, it is interesting to compare a number of differing viewpoints on the subject of aging and its cause and effect.

The Traditional Medicine Viewpoint

Gerontologists, medical scientists specializing in the aging process, have yet to agree on the biological processes that underlie aging. Among the many theories are the **worn template concept**, wherein every time cells divide, the copying mechanism is more likely to introduce errors; the **accumulated toxins theory**, wherein the body is gradually poisoned by the accumulation of chemicals it cannot excrete; and the **immune surveillance theory**, which postulates a progressive decline in the immune system's ability to detect and destroy microorganisms and developing tumors.

The Alternative Health Viewpoint

The aging process is a combination of many changes. For example, **internal body clocks** switch off functions, slowing the production of a number of important hormones, causing the immune system to weaken, resulting in less resistance to illness. There is also **general wear and tear** on the body from the sun's ultraviolet light, pollution, drugs, and pesticides, together with the **physical exertions of life**, all of which cause the formation of highly active atoms or atom groups that react with others to damage body cells and protein fibers (collagen). In turn, that leads to **cross-linking**, resulting in protein fibers becoming tangled, causing a number of deteriorations such as the skin losing its suppleness, wrinkles developing, veins and arteries hardening, muscles softening, and limbs stiffening. However, research shows that some primitive tribes living on sparse diets of natural foods, such as fish and grain, live to advanced ages and enjoy good health and energy not troubled by the Western diseases of degeneration such as arthritis and heart disorders.

Nutrition may therefore play an important role in healthy longevity.

Long before the final acceptance of being as old as your age and functioning at a true-to-self level, millions of people throughout the world devote a large proportion of their lives, and many parts of their bodies, to a never-ending, quixotic quest to halt or at least slow the dreaded aging process. It is a complete reversal of their pre-teen and teenage years, with the idea now being to try to cheat the aging process by looking younger than one's age.

Plastic surgery is perhaps the most drastic means of trying to reverse the aging process, but it is not the preferred choice of most, nor is it the choice for those who could not care less about being a cut above the rest. Plastic surgery is, of course, but one of many options in the battle against the aging process. Other options include transplants, implants, native plants, false parts, artificial bits and pieces, pills, tablets, potions, and a host of practitioners with myriad suggestions and remedies.

Certainly, there are good arguments both for and against the efforts of so many to hang onto what they think is their younger self—their Peter Pan persona. However, just as certain is the role played by the mind in many aspects of the aging process.

Like so many other aspects of life, decade development, and dealing with the recurring questions, **state of mind** is either a person's major strength or major weakness. To witness the way people condition themselves for a rapid aging process decline, listen for oft-repeated statements that are, in reality, negative affirmations!

1. *"I guess I'm just getting too old."*
2. *"I'm really starting to feel my age."*
3. *"I feel I'm aging before my time."*
4. *"What can you expect at my age?"*

When forty or fifty-year-olds repeatedly utter such phrases, they are preparing their minds and bodies to react eventually to the suggestions. The negative self-talk conditioning is not restricted to older age groups. It can start in the early thirties, with utterances such as:

- *"I'd better do it now before I get too old."*
- *"I should have done it when I was younger."*

To dismiss the destructive effect that negative self-talk can generate is to dismiss the well-documented success of positive affirmations, resolutions, and prayers.

The age difference between two people is a subject responsible for a wide variety of conflicting viewpoints. The wider the age gap, the more it will be influenced by the 10-

You Are Only as Old as Your Age

Year Glitch. For example, one partner will be in a different decade phase of growth and development, and that can lead to a number of challenges requiring more give and take than normal.

There is one age-related expression capable of leading to a healthy, productive, and contented aging process. Living by its creed enables a birthday to be far more influential than a once-a-year celebration. Adopting the expression as a permanent state of mind acts as both a guide for the now and a warning about expending time, energy, money, and emotion on age-past or age-future. To enjoy all of its proven benefits at any time in a life span and to avoid fretting for what is going or gone or fearing for what is coming, simply learn how to **act your age!**

The 10-Year Glitch

CHAPTER THIRTEEN

Wake up to Your Dream

Three distinct phases contribute to the momentum of the earthly experience:
- *Learning from the past*
- *Living in the now*
- *Planning for the future*

The three phases have a common denominator in that each can be influenced by the power of dreams. Coincidentally, there are three types of dreams, any of which can be experienced individually or collectively during any one of the phases.

The future-driven dream is conducted during the awakened stage, having as its propelling force motivations such as affirmations, ardent desires, and prayers. Whether the future-driven dream can be achieved during the sleep process is a matter for conjecture, but it certainly provides much material for learned discussion and debate. Stories about people who have dreamed the winner of a horse race prior to the race or dreamed the winning lottery numbers prior to the draw add romanticism to the subject, but they also tend to cloud the issue of whether it is humanly possible to experience something in the present that will happen in the future!

What is possible, of course, is that facts about the horse and the race or a variety of oft-used numbers can surface during a dream in the way any other data, ideas, or material can surface. However, whereas most sleep-induced dream material is discarded, a dream that might possibly lead to a financial windfall is treated with a degree of significance and awe it rarely deserves.

One orthodox medical viewpoint states that dreaming can be seen as a parallel process in which the mental impressions, feelings, and ideas taken in during the day are sorted out. The content of dreams, therefore, closely represents the day's preoccupations, with the impressions, ideas, and feelings distorted by the lack of conscious mind reasoning.

That explanation provides a strong argument against being able to experience a future-driven dream during the sleeping stage. Conversely, it can also mean that if a person spends time in an awakened state developing a dream motivated by affirmations, ardent desires, or prayer, ultimately the dream could be duplicated and surface as a sleep-induced dream.

The late Walt Disney, one of the great dream creators and developers, gave the world one of its most potent universal truths when he explained his success by saying, *"If you can dream it, you can do it."* How often does a person achieving some kind of award or accolade respond by saying, *"This is something I've always dreamed about!"*?

One confusing aspect of future-driven dreams during the awakened state is the well-documented case histories of people "seeing" future events or happenings. Examples would include an architect who sees a building in his mind's eye long before it becomes a reality on the drawing board or computer screen or the artist who pictures a completed work before a brushstroke is made or a hammer and chisel strike the first blow of a sculpture. It would also include an author's mind, which is often filled with the plot and characters for a novel long before the first word of the first chapter is written, and inventors who see a working model of their creation long before a prototype is completed.

The bond linking the foregoing is a powerful and wonderful function of the mind called **visualization.** It is a function available to all but used by few, because it is closely allied to the mind functions of **imagination** and **creativity**. Although visualization is often linked to future-driven dreams, it is far more compatible and understood when linked with imagination and creativity, both of which function in the awakened state.

Clairvoyance provides yet another angle to future-driven dream analysis, but it is treated in a coy manner by mainstream thinking, which describes clairvoyance as follows: *The faculty of seeing mentally what is out of sight.*

The second type of dream is called ***the strange dream***, in which a wide variety of logical and illogical impressions are mixed and mingled in a haphazard fantasy of sometimes-epic proportions. Past (often very past) events, people, and places are freely juxtaposed with current happenings, leading to a result that enables the dreamer to fly, hide, climb, dangle, race, cry, laugh, lose, find, win, survive, and triumph.

People talk about this type of dream because it was too strange to be true, and it does provide interesting material for amateur analysis. Other people are also interested in hearing about the strange type of dream because it is the most common and therefore can be shared without too much self-revelation—unlike the third type of dream.

The 10-Year Glitch

The past-driven dream is often a recurring dream that derives its impetus from highly personal data. Because of the personal aspect, it is a dream not freely discussed with other people. It can be the dream from which nightmares evolve! If the need to reveal the contents of the dream becomes necessary, it is usually with a dream analyst. This modality type is becoming more respected as life becomes increasingly complex, with the mind called upon to expand its boundaries, the memory to store more data, and the sub-conscious to decipher more information.

The past-driven dream exists because most, if not all, humans have at least one secret they would not under any circumstances reveal to people close to them, let alone to the world at large. The secret (or secrets) can be as harmless as a mild fantasy or as damaging as a bizarre fantasy considered taboo by current society standards. This area is the domain of the dark secret harbored by the **undetected** alcoholic, gambler, embezzler, drug addict, and law breaker. All would be victims of this particular dream, and all will eventually suffer the torment of the dream becoming a recurring nightmare.

Detection is often the only way for the cycle to be broken. All attempts to memory-hide or bury the problem inevitably fail. **Conscious excuses** can be used to justify the actions during the awakened stage, but the same conscious function is unable to work in the sleeping state.

Guilt, shame, and embarrassment during the awakened stage, along with any number of other psychologically damaging effects, are the by-products of this type of dream.

One unfortunate aspect stemming from the past-driven dream is that a victim of the dream's nightmare influence may not have contributed to the cause of the problem. Although a spouse, partner, or friend of the guilty party is innocent, the repercussions following detection can often lead to the same fear and apprehension experienced by the perpetrator. The recurring question of life, *Should I feel guilty?* is one that could haunt the innocent unless dismissed as soon as possible.

A simple but highly effective technique can be used for the first and second type of dream. **Looking back on life** on a regular basis is as good a way as any is when endeavoring to achieve a desired quality of life while living in the moment. The fifth decade of the 10-Year Glitch is the **evaluation decade**, in which people must look back to see if they have lost sight of their dreams, goals, or aspirations.

One of the more tiresome, often destructive, and overly materialistic dictates of modern society is the constant urging to plan. Myriad future-based schemes (and scams) have been created that promote a **fear-of-the-future message** as a means of securing a successful outcome for the promoters.

Of course, there is a place, reason, and ultimate reward for adopting the plan-for-the-future directive. But if the adoption becomes slavish and obsessional, the inestimable value of living in the moment is ignored or lost. Once it is lost, the luxury of having the time and inclination to look back occasionally at life is also lost, along with many positive attributes unobtainable in any other way!

Too much emphasis on future planning and thinking can often lead to an identity crisis, because the future keeps arriving so fast that living in the present becomes a blurred incident between past and future. Oft-repeated utterances, such as *"I don't know where the time goes"* or *"I don't seem to have time to myself anymore"* can serve as a warning sign that an unhealthy preoccupation with the future is counteracting many of the life-enhancing pleasures and benefits obtained from living in the present.

Looking back on one's life at least once a year can identify aspects of living that perhaps require some kind of adjustment, realignment, correction, elimination, or improvement, or it may simply supply the confidence-boosting acknowledgment that all is on track. Looking back should not be confused with *"living in the past,"* however, because doing so is every bit as counterproductive as attempting to mentally live life in the future. When applied to the dream types, looking back can be as quick as a short review (if all is well) or as long as it takes for a full-scale analysis if life in that moment is bogged down with indecision, stemming from minor or major problems that appear to have no immediate solution.

When confronted with the recurring question of life, *Am I where I should be?* it is generally a mistake to **look ahead** for the answer.

If a person is unhappy, disappointed, or frustrated because of not being where he/she wanted to be, then looking back should be the preferred option for solution seeking. The recurring question, *Am I where I should be?* applies to relationships, careers, social circles, living conditions, and any other aspect of current life affecting quality of living at the moment.

Attempting to change a less-than-favorable situation is not going to be a successful venture when searching for a solution in the future. Although that comment appears to be stating the obvious, it is surprising how many people keep hoping their current situation will simply go away if they keep wishfully thinking and hoping for a future-initiated solution.

People are products of their pasts, not of their futures.

Therefore, any obstacle or hindrance encountered in the present is usually a continuation of something started in the past, which can readily be identified and corrected by looking back rather than looking ahead. Any person asking, *"Why is this happening again?"* need look no further than personal history for an answer to this question and a solution to the problem.

Trying to correct a problem that has roots in the past with a future-driven dream will only result in wasted affirmations, ardent desires, and prayers. Looking ahead when they should have looked back is perhaps the single most common reason why many people never have their future-driven dreams fulfilled.

Without a doubt, the most beneficial gain from regular use of the **looking-back-on-life technique** occurs in the areas of talent, ability, and potential especially if the foregoing attributes have been intentionally allowed to lapse, or circumstances beyond one's control have caused development of the attributes to cease.

Many reasons exist for people having to put a special talent, ability, or potential on hold. Then, coupled with being caught in the whirlpool of life known as the **plan-for-the-future syndrome**, the attribute is shelved or otherwise lost and forgotten.

Looking back on life to when conditions or circumstances were changed naturally or deliberately can help to rediscover, and remove the dust covers from, the dormant talent, ability, or potential. From that moment, the future-driven dream will become a powerful force in making up for lost time and opportunity, thus giving the attributes a fresh new lease on life.

At various stages of the 10-Year Glitch, the level of achievement and contentment will greatly depend on the time and effort expended on the potent exercise of reflective thinking. What could be better than knowing the direction life's journey is taking, especially when it is in the direction that the traveler intended?

Naturally, not all journeys are straightforward. Deviations can lead to a loss of direction, but the occasional effort to look

The 10-Year Glitch

back on life is the ideal way to identify those sometimes subtle deviations.

Look back now—what view do you see?

Chapter Fourteen

What on Earth Are We Doing Here?

Is life's earthly experience becoming so complicated, complex, and obscure that the question of life's purpose is becoming ever more difficult to answer? A rapidly increasing number of people worldwide are enlisting the aid of a life coach in a bid to make sense of the completely bewildering event. The steady growth and development of the life coach profession is definitely a sign of the times. A recent comment in an international publication stated that if the 1980s put therapy on the mainstream map, and the 1990's, complementary medicine, then the 2001–2010 decade will surely see life coaching make it to the mainstream big time.

Sport, of course, has long functioned with coaches who accept the responsibility of motivating, guiding, and generally encouraging their charges to strive for their highest performance capabilities. The life coach fulfills a similar function on behalf of clients, with the difference being that the game of life is the challenge, and the reward for victory is the discovery of a personal purpose within that life. However, unlike the typical image of a sports coach, the life coach will not rant, rave, or berate when things do not go according to a carefully formulated game plan. Rather, the life coach will use a combination of skills that include counseling, motivation, mentoring, life management, and spiritual guidance. Appreciating the reason for the development of life coaches requires an understanding of just how difficult it has become to channel thoughts, energy, and focus into a single life purpose.

A question at a motivation seminar asked attendees to supply a reason for their purpose in life. The widespread and varied responses provided perfect examples of why a **single purpose** can be extremely elusive. The more popular responses included:

- *To be rich*
- *To be famous*
- *To be successful*
- *To be able to do anything I want when I want to do it*
- *To be my own person, answerable to no one*

Money, acquisition, and ownership in one form or another were the most oft-repeated and desired options for a life of purpose. At face value, they could be considered (and perhaps condemned) as being selfish responses. However, they are simply the pre-conditioned responses to self-indulging, personal gratification messages received continually in this modern, materialistic earthly experience environment. That environment does not lend itself to a straightforward solution to the life's purpose question. A seemingly clear-cut, single purpose early in life will require many decisions to be made and obstacles to be overcome if it is to remain the sole driving force throughout a lifetime.

What on Earth Are We Doing Here?

For a limited few, that does not apply. For those humans who invent, create, discover, or otherwise contribute to the quality-of-life development of the earthly experience, it would seem their purpose in life was **pre-determined.** Think of the genius composers; the heroic adventurers who conquered land, sea and air; the medical scientists who developed life-saving and enhancing medical procedures and cures—how fortunate they were to be gifted with a single, often all-consuming, purpose in life. Some, of course, paid a severe personal price for the opportunity given to them. In some instances, the discovery of their life's purpose was achieved despite their best efforts to avoid it! Many of the saints, kings and queens, military leaders, and world leaders revealed their enormous strengths of character after a leadership role was thrust upon them.

For most people, a life purpose choice is often in place early in life. At that stage, the family environment plays a pivotal role in the direction of the decision. A life purpose can be either encouraged, and thus flourish, or discouraged, and thus perish.

A positive family atmosphere allows flexible thinking and attitudes that in turn encourage the birth of a life's purpose. It allows an individual *"to be."* It gives the individual free, unrestricted opportunities to explore, to seek, to challenge, and ultimately to realize and release talent and potential via a gift from the universe known as **freedom of expression**. That freedom is surely the first step in recognizing, and then setting, a life's purpose in place.

One certain way of checking whether a life's purpose is in place is to ask the question: *If I could start again, would I change anything?*

For many people, change is something to be avoided if possible. When linked to a life purpose or a reason for the earthly experience, however, the ability and courage to accept the need for change is an essential element in achieving a harmonious quality of life.

The 10-Year Glitch

Change is often forced upon people via a crisis. There are many well-documented cases of people discovering their true vocation, their spiritual (or true) self, or their real purpose for living following a crisis at some point in their lives. Prior to the crisis, these same people had been aware of beliefs beyond mainstream acceptance, but they chose to ignore the obvious because it would mean a change, often a drastic change, in their life's direction.

The reward for surviving a crisis and accepting the new awareness is the *total understanding of their life's purpose!* So few ever get to experience that comforting, tranquil feeling, and yet the universe has supplied the ways and means for almost any person to achieve what is considered an ideal state of being.

Without doubt, life's great journey can be either a rough ride or a reasonably comfortable one. Knowing the purpose of the journey and being in control of how to reach its destination is one way of determining the quality of the earthly experience. It will also help to prepare for the occasional detour that is an inevitable element in the journey. One habit worth adopting as a countermeasure to an unwanted detour is to enlist the aid of the recurring question, *Am I where I should be?*

When the question is applied to relationships, social circles, jobs, or careers, a detour will not last for long or make it too difficult to return to the chosen route. This technique is particularly effective during the annual life adjustment most people indulge in called the New Year's resolution. It is a time when comments such as *"I must get my life back on track"* or *"I must get my life in order"* are indications that a life purpose has been lost or at least misplaced temporarily.

The beginning of a new year is, for many people, a time when life's purpose comes sharply into focus. Much of life's irritations, along with the anxiety, pain, and suffering endured by people, are usually due to an unwillingness (or fear) to end an unsatisfactory element in their life. The recurring question,

What on Earth Are We Doing Here?

When should I say it is over? inevitably arises on or near the start of a new year.

Attempting to start or re-charge a purpose in life will be extremely difficult if energy is drained and focus clouded due to stress-inducing circumstances that could and should have been eliminated. Failure to correct the situation will invariably lead to one of the saddest comments any human can make: *"My life is without purpose."*

This comment often follows the end of some useful contribution that has been accepted as a life's purpose. When it ends for one reason or another, a fear is immediately released that finds its outlet in the debilitating comment. The fear stems from the recurring question, *Can I start again?*

Or, put another way, can I find a new purpose in life? Of all the challenges faced during the earthly experience, this question is perhaps one of the easier ones to answer, because the element of experience is there to help. All that is needed is the desire to create a new, worthwhile life purpose and the *determination to begin it without fearing the future!*

Having a life purpose firmly in place results in personal freedom as one of its greatest rewards, and freedom, in its variety of forms, is a highly desirable condition of the earthly experience. Unfortunately, it is also elusive, almost to the point of being unobtainable, for many people. The reason lies in the human penchant for allowing all manner of external influences to restrict the attainment of being wholly free in mind, body, and spirit.

As with many other aspects of life, the desire to achieve a particular life purpose must start with self-motivation. Therefore, a desire for freedom of expression in thought, word, and deed, absolute essentials in any life purpose, cannot be obtained if an individual is a victim of other people's opinions, wishes, criticisms, or manipulations.

The 10-Year Glitch

The way to overcome such a negative situation is to live life according to personally chosen standards, values, and beliefs. In doing so, a purpose in life can achieve its full and ultimate freedom of expression—the unencumbered, life-enhancing freedom that gives substance and solidarity to any genuine purpose in life.

A common way in which people lose sight of, or endanger, their purpose in life is the misuse of **time**, the most precious and valuable asset obtainable from the universe. Time can be a friend in the pursuit of an honorable purpose in life or a mortal enemy where no purpose exists.

In the absence of a life purpose requiring the traditional idea of owning, collecting, succeeding, or achieving in a materialistic manner, an alternative life purpose can be equally as fulfilling and ultimately more rewarding.

A life lived without regret is perhaps the most selfless purpose that it is possible to achieve in an earthly lifetime experience. To come to the end of life's great journey and to be able to say, *"I have no regrets"* would compare favorably to any other life purpose imaginable.

First, to understand and appreciate why is to acknowledge the insidious mental condition created by regret, and secondly, to accept why it is so important to answer in a positive manner the recurring question, *Should I feel guilty?*

Regret is a mind condition that can be obvious, but it can also lodge surreptitiously in the mind and create all kinds of havoc when it comes to health, happiness, and a desire for a meaningful purpose in life. Side effects of the condition can include anger, frustration, and loss of self-esteem, along with stress-related conditions such as anxiety, fear, and a loss of control over a life's purpose. On the other hand, a life without regrets—*what on earth could be a better life purpose than that?*

Chapter Fifteen

The View is Clear From an Open Mind

Historical facts record how the **closed-mind mentality**, often started and then prolonged by narrow-minded and dogmatic religions, has been responsible for years of hostility and blood-shedding conflict between nations. However, the destructive closed-mind thought process is not restricted to the international arena. It also creates spiteful antagonism whenever people encounter each other. Relatives, partners, neighbors, committee members, and that person you cannot stand can all find themselves victims of the closed-mind mentality. It is interesting to compare a variety of doors with a variety of mind types as a way of illustrating how quality of life is often related to the quality of thoughts.

The trapdoor mind is the ultimate closed mind.

To identify it, listen for the oft-repeated utterance, *"That's the way I am, and I'm not going to change for anyone, so if people don't like it, that's their problem."* Thus is created a perfect excuse to act in a rude, offensive, tactless, ignorant, selfish, stubborn, or boorish manner. When the trapdoor mind is the dominating force of a nation, company, union, household, or committee, then compromise, conciliation, or any form of objective communication is non-existent. The trapdoor mind attitude is *"Fall in with my views, or stay locked out."*

The roller-door mind is not far removed from the trapdoor mind, but it is not as destructive.

It appears to be open and receptive, but the moment it is confronted with a new or alternative idea or a change in the status quo, down comes the protective barrier. The roller-door mind will invariably say "no" rather than "yes" if saying "yes" means change. It fails to take advantage of opportunities and usually condemns all forms of progress initiative.

The sliding-door mind goes too far the other way, with change forever taking place.

Open and closed, backward and forward, never open or closed for too long, it is also known as the busy mind, constantly subjected to whims, fancies, and myriad non-productive thoughts. A sliding-door mentality is evident when a person is constantly announcing that he or she is flat-out busy when, in reality, achieving very little productivity due to being disorganized.

The cuckoo-clock mind is identified with the utterance, "I'm not afraid to say what I think, because if I think it should be said, then I will say it!"

And they do, ad infinitum, every hour on the hour, sounding like the little bird but not as interesting.

The barn-door mind is a mind too wide open and, therefore, vulnerable.

In striving to achieve an open-minded attitude, it is well to be aware that too open can be as destructive as too closed. Psychologists believe that most people have a healthy mental defense mechanism that helps them retain control of their minds.

In the late 1960's and early 1970's, a plethora of Indian gurus encouraged devotees to relinquish the defense mechanism in order to open their minds to the wonders of Eastern philosophies. Eventually, it was discovered that a number of the gurus were nothing more than greedy, dishonest opportunists more interested in opening the wallets and purses of their devotees rather than their minds. Sri Karunanda, a genuine and much-revered guru of those times, issued this warning to his followers: *"For a closed mind, the silence will soon fill with false voices and respond to its secret pride, vanity, ambition, lust, greed, or desire."*

The main argument against a barn-door mind is that any space filled beyond its capacity will ultimately split, fracture, crack, or burst.

The security-door mind is usually found in a variety of medical circles.

Over the past couple of decades, there has been an increasing awareness of and interest in preventative and alternative/complementary healing methods, along with an acceptance of the value of vitamins and natural substances in diets and nutrition. The majority of medical practitioners cautiously observed the developments by looking through the peephole of their security-door mind. Nowadays, with complementary healing methods firmly established, many general practitioners have replaced the peephole with a security chain, enabling them to get a better view of the development, albeit from a narrow perspective.

The revolving-door mind is perhaps the ideal open-mind mentality.

The most satisfying reward obtained from an open-minded attitude is the ability and desire to hear, evaluate, and respond to both sides of any issues. The revolving door caters to an orderly and consistent ebb and flow, allowing for a full, unrestricted view of both sides at the same time. It cannot be slammed shut regardless of any sudden adverse change in circumstances.

An additional teaching of Sri Karunanda makes an ideal closing for the door and mind comparison: *"An open mind allows truth, tolerance, and clarity of vision to flourish."*

Chapter Sixteen

Worthy of Imitation

Whenever there is a general mood of unrest in various sections of society, it usually indicates a serious concern about a number of social issues. The common cry invariably pinpoints lack of respect, discipline, and responsible behavior, particularly toward long-established, cherished, and stable bastions of society, as the major ignition factors for the flare-up of mainstream anger and irritation.

One popular and regular method for airing grievances and voicing disapproval is talkback radio programs, but they rarely provide any answers or solutions. Instead, a rash of generalizations, blanket statements, or wildly inaccurate accusations is bandied about in the hope of hitting a target. Invariably, the target becomes today's youth!

Is this a recently developed phenomenon? Consider this critique on the subject by philosopher Socrates from 400 B.C.: *"Our youth loves luxury. They have bad manners, contempt for authority; show disrespect for their elders and love to chatter in places of exercise. Children are the tyrants not the servants of their households. They no longer rise when their elders enter the room.*

The 10-Year Glitch

They contradict their parents, chatter before company, gobble food and tyrannize teachers."

That statement, of course, was made before the creation of the Department of Youth and Community Services, a government department that elevated the rights of children to levels defying logic, common sense, or believability!

Complaining, criticizing, and protesting without supplying or at least suggesting remedial possibilities are lazy, unproductive approaches to solving problems. If, as perceived by many adults, today's youth are responsible for causing some of society's current aberrations, are those same adults blameless? Certainly, the youth of today are the future of the nation, but the adults of today should be supplying an extremely important element that is fundamental to the well-being of any nation.

Individually, **role** means, *"one's task or function,"* and **model** means, *"object of imitation."* When combined, **role model** becomes a powerful unit capable of either inspiration or destruction. It exerts a direct influence on the emotional, logical, and spiritual senses of all human beings but remains largely ignored or vastly underestimated in comparison to other aspects of influence.

The role model influence (good or bad) starts in early childhood, with the initial role models being parents, older brothers or sisters, other relatives, and teachers. Ideal role models teach and encourage by example and can inspire an impressionable mind to imitate what it sees and hears. Most adults can immediately recall their early role models (good or bad), and most will now be either positively applying what they accepted as a youngster or continually fighting to overcome the negative influence.

Co-author of this book, Margot Maurice, details here her own experience of the role model subject.

Worthy of Imitation

I have had three very strong role models in my life, namely my grandmother, my mother, and an inspirational woman named Isobel.

My grandmother on my mother's side was a very strong Taurean Scotswoman who became responsible for much of my early upbringing because my mother worked during the World War II years (as did many women at that time).

Grandmother encouraged me in many positive ways, with a notable example being her advice that I could do anything I set my heart on doing. She planted the seed in my young mind that I should totally believe in myself and was there to champion me in every endeavor I undertook.

My mother, on the other hand, didn't have much influence in my life until after my grandmother died. I always felt my mother was content to be in the shadow of her mother, happy in the way I was developing as a child under grandmother's tutelage and guidance.

My mother readily accepted the role model mantle and soon displayed her own strengths of character in carrying on the job of my positive development. In turn, in her later years, I used grandmother's philosophies to foster my mother's desire for independence and encouraged her to join various voluntary organizations. In her late seventies, she started

The 10-Year Glitch

> a computer course and became computer adept, while many others in her age group decided that particular area of life was beyond their capabilities and comprehension. My mother remained active and contributed to life right up to the time she died, and she was a great example of how a positive role model can be such a life-enhancing influence.
>
> My other great role model, Isobel, was a human dynamo throughout a life that lasted well into her nineties. It was during her late eighties that Isobel finished and published a book detailing her life's work as a homoeopath and radionics specialist.
>
> Because of the influence and example set by those three role models, I now enjoy an active life in which I am as retired as I want to be, as busy as I choose to be, and, hopefully, a good role model for my daughter and granddaughter.

A wonderful example of how a role model can affect people on a **worldwide scale** was illustrated in the life and times of a young woman who became known as the People's Princess.

Tragically, it was only after Princess Diana's death that her role model value was realized and fully appreciated.

For millions of children (and adults still young at heart), Diana represented the real-life princess of timeless fairy stories—beautiful, charming, an effervescent personality projected through a warm, expansive, ever-present smile. Diana was a caring person with the unselfish desire and ability to highlight the suffering of human beings that the rest of the world had forgotten or simply ignored.

Princess Diana was vulnerable—a ready target for pseudo-righteous forces, but her resilience enabled her to thwart their machinations. To dislike her meant a flaw in one's ability to assess attributes **worthy of imitation**.

The display of universal public grieving highlighted an element in human nature that is often a cause for regret, which in turn can evolve into guilt. *"You don't know what you've got / 'til it's gone"* was how Joni Mitchell expressed the element in her song "Big Yellow Taxi." In other words, praise, appreciate, thank, forgive, and encourage now, before it is too late! It is a guaranteed way to avoid being haunted by the recurring question of life, *Should I feel guilty?*

The people teenagers choose as role models often horrify adults, especially parents.

Specialists in adolescent phases of behavior suggest that choosing role models not approved by adults is a way of breaking the shackles of dependence. Music is a perfect **short-term** vehicle, because the young performers are themselves rebelling against adult society constraints and can promote that via dress, behavior, attitude, and song lyrics.

Ultimately, the teenager will come out of the phase and begin yearning for role models able to supply attributes suitable for **long-term** aspirations. One positive technique people can use to overcome the recurring question, *Should I fear the future?* is to become their own role model.

Almost every human being is capable of living up to positive character attributes that already reside within their psyche. The positive character traits are highly suitable for role model status. Unfortunately, counteracting the potential for constructive contribution is a particularly virulent human characteristic that first stifles, and ultimately suffocates, the attributes.

Knocking is the colloquial name for the characteristic. It is also known as *"the tall poppy syndrome."* The affiliates of knocking include disparaging, unwarranted, or ill-informed criticism, malicious gossip, spiteful innuendo, and the denigration of achievers and achievement.

Knocking reveals the inner self in the worst possible light because envy, jealousy, or inadequacy is its prime motivation. Eliminating the aberration is an essential step in allowing the role model attributes to blossom and serve their purpose. When individuals become their own role models, it is not only a sign of true achievement. It also allows them, by example, to become role models for others and people **worthy of imitation.**

CHAPTER SEVENTEEN

A Rare and Precious Gift

"Oh, the comfort, the inexpressible comfort of feeling safe with a person, having neither to weigh thoughts nor measure words…"

With that poignant thought, author, poet, and philosopher George Eliot provided what has become accepted as the definitive description of **true friendship**. French writer Andre Malraux expressed a similar sentiment with his observation that the difficult thing is not to stand by your friends when they are right, but when they are wrong.

There are people who claim they have many, many friends, whereas human behavioral science data indicates that if a person has **five true friends** in their lifetime, they have been blessed. True friendship has a pivotal element that distances itself from the more shallow relationships that often masquerade as friendship. Qualities such as faithfulness, trustworthiness, loyalty, and respect are all essential ingredients in the friends-and-friendship mix. Most people will expect their friends to be endowed with these qualities, but to obtain the true friendship status as described by Eliot, the mix must contain the pivotal characteristic of **constancy**—*a component of a relationship between variables that does not change its value.*

In many human interactions, the lack of constancy is the single most destructive element when seeking longevity. True friendship, like true love or any other true facet of life, develops endurance because what is good and wholesome in the beginning is not subject to continual variation. It remains unchanged regardless of disruption, complications, or a shift in circumstances. The inability of some adults to inject the element of constancy into their relationships, like many other adult aberrations, can be traced back to childhood.

Children are notorious for their lack of friendship constancy. An unshakeable, deep-seated, very best allegiance can last only a matter of days. In children, the lack of constancy is healthy because they are simply expressing **truth in friendship**. A very best friend who *"does the wrong thing"* is immediately banished and quickly replaced with the very best friend who was banished the week before.

Adults, on the other hand, will overlook, ignore, or forgive all manner of sleights and wrongdoings *"for the sake of the friendship."* That is **deception in friendship** and can result in highly unhealthy and manipulative types of relationships. Conversely, deception as practiced by children is not a serious matter because it is done with genuine innocence.

When Mary is asked why she is crying, she replies, *"My best friend broke my tennis racket."* When asked how it happened, she says, *"I hit her with it."*

When Tom is admonished for kicking Billy in the stomach, he protests by saying, *"It wasn't my fault; Billy turned around too quickly."*

A Rare and Precious Gift

The following two questions continue to cause vexation regardless of much answer-seeking analysis and dissection. Is it possible to achieve true friendship between parents and their children, or between adult males and females?

True friendship is not corrupted by dominance, manipulation, competitiveness, or autocracy. Nor is it tainted by any type of emotional blackmail designed to create anger, fear, regret, or guilt. If it was possible to eliminate all the foregoing friendship-destroying obstacles and replace them with a constant application of positive, non-confrontational elements, then yes, parents and their children could achieve true friendship early in their relationship, but would it be a healthy situation?

When children begin the push for independence, a major step is the severing of dependency ties with their parents, which is a natural course toward conflict. Far better, then, for parents and their children to develop **mutual respect** during the formative years, because true friendship is a derivative of mutual respect and therefore will surface in later years.

A variety of theories exists as to why it is difficult for many males and females to become true friends. The difficulty of overcoming sexual overtones is the most popular and readily accepted theory. However, the theory is a flaccid one compared to a number of other theories put forward as reasons for the corruption and tainting of true friendship between members of the opposite sex. Lack of trust, possessiveness, and suspicion are the most destructive elements.

What is the Secret of a Happy Marriage?

That question was put to a wide variety of couples all considered to have a long and successful marriage. Interestingly, **being each other's best friend** was the common reason given by survey participants, and most said they had enjoyed a friendship-type relationship from the day they had first started dating.

Two truisms reveal an essential element in the friends-and-friendship formula:

- *"When you're in trouble, you find out who your true friends are."*
- *"A friend in need is a friend indeed."*

One person unselfishly and unconditionally coming to the aid of another is, of course, the foundation upon which true friendship is built. Unfortunately, there is also the type of person who seems to be in permanent need. They are generally adults who have not successfully bridged the gap between childhood dependence and adult independence. This results in their making excessive demands for attention and help from others, putting them into a category of **co-dependence**. Providing they have a friend who is a chronic co-dependent, the friendship will survive because they are satisfying each other's quality-of-life requirements: one needs someone, and the other needs to be needed. True friendship can certainly flow from such a relationship.

A not-so-healthy situation arises when a **normal** friend becomes the **victim** of excessive demands. People finding themselves in such a situation should take an assertive stance and end the friendship, because one of the major causes of stress illness can be traced to what is now called **friendship abuse**. The term **long-suffering** has its origin in this area.

A Rare and Precious Gift

Like so many other worthy aspects of life, becoming your own best friend is a pursuit worth achieving, because the ability to create true friendship is a rare and precious gift.

The 10-Year Glitch

CHAPTER EIGHTEEN

The Space Where Earth and Spirit Meet

The generation gap is but one of many gaps that often keep people together physically but wide apart mentally. There are many theories on ways to either close or at least narrow the gap between generations, with the ultimate aim being to develop and promote communication and interaction between the generations. Usually, the good-intentioned efforts of a variety of experts fall short of their objectives, because society actually survives and indeed flourishes by keeping gaps open!

Although the **generation gap** is the best known, there are now a number of other gaps challenging its long-standing dominance. Vested interests in the shape of politicians, corporate moguls, and giant corporations, along with a host of other society manipulators, have become adept at appearing to be doing something about the inequitable balance associated with the current crop of gaps.

A good example of such machinations and one of the more obvious, ongoing, and frustrating is the gap that separates the

The 10-Year Glitch

thinking and attitude of traditional healing methods toward alternative or complementary healing techniques. In 1942, Doctor Frederick W. Bailes, hopeful that the gap was closing, offered this observation.

> *"The practice of mental and spiritual healing is coming more and more into its rightful place in our daily lives. The more forward-looking physicians are investigating it and others are practicing it even when they dare not publicize the fact. The physician of the future will be a person who corrects the thought-life of the patient, thus treating the cause instead of dosing the effect."*

Decades later, there are still many patients who dare not reveal to their family doctor that they have tried or are receiving some form of alternative healing, are taking nutritional supplements, or are embracing some complementary modality.

Vague promises and faint hearts cannot close gaps that require bridging, covering, closing, filling, or sealing. Gaps that separate the rich and poor, young and old, good and evil, along with the wide divergence of views associated with issues covering ideology, race, and the environment, are invariably treated as individual problems when they should be treated in conjunction with a gap that encompasses all other gaps.

The gap considered a universal core of any society is known as the **20/80 gap**. It derives its being from the philosophy that 20% of any society directs, controls, and otherwise provides for the other 80%. This includes the supply of food, clothing, and shelter, the three basic essentials of life.

Leaders and followers, haves and have-nots, the establishment and the masses, are the most common titles used to distinguish the two groups. Although seeming to be an imbalance, the 20/80 ratio is, in fact, the perfect balance for a stable, harmonious society. While that balance is maintained, the society functions with a minimum of fuss or disruption.

Trouble arises when factions of the masses attempt to **jump the gap** in search of a more favorable share of power and possessions. The rebellion loses impetus when the factions realize it takes any number of special talents and attributes to be part of the 20%. These attributes include self-discipline, wisdom, vision, and courage, together with, in some instances, a degree of devious manipulative skills that are used only *"for the good of the masses."*

The truth is that a society must naturally have more followers than leaders. Therefore, more effort (and money) is expended on discouraging **gap jumpers** by making the gaps even wider. Joseph E. Levine, the great Hollywood film director, neatly explained the process with a twist of an old truism.

"You can fool all the people all of the time if the advertising is right and the budget is big enough."

In theory, it is, of course, possible for any person to make the move from the eighty-percent masses to the twenty-percent elite, but there is a strict gap-crossing procedure to follow in order to make the move a long-term event. It is accomplished by way of yet another of life's intriguing gaps: the gap between the **actual self** and the **imagined self.**

- *How to close the gap is one of the major challenges of the earthly experience.*

- *The actual self is where a person is now…in the present.*

- *The imagined self is where a person would like to be in the future.*

Success in one form or another is the result of closing the gap and bonding the two selves. The surest way to achieve the bonding is to follow a formula that has stood the test of time: *"Success happens when preparation meets opportunity."* Every human has a gap that will help to either accomplish the bonding of the two selves or prevent it from happening.

The gap between the ears is a life-enhancing component for some and a liability for others. Listing just a few of the contradictory elements for which the gap between the ears is responsible illustrates how vital it is to understand its function and the way to develop it as an ally before it becomes an enemy. The gap allows the generation-gap tradition to continue, whereby the young know all, the middle deny all, and the old alibi all.

The gap causes millions of dollars to be spent on research and development into drugs and methods to treat physical complaints, while patients with **physical** problems caused by **mental** aberrations occupy one in three hospital beds. The gap enables 20% of a society to act as judge, jury, and executioner in any trial of strength with the masses. The gap keeps the masses content due to a mistaken belief that the will of the people can at any time alter or change the status quo or the future course of events.

- *The gap creates reasons for succeeding or excuses for failing.*
- *The gap can maintain peace or start a war, build a monastery or bomb a village.*
- *The gap can allow love and devotion to flourish or hate and revenge to fester.*
- *The gap can kill or cure.*

The Space Where Earth and Spirit Meet

Some people fill the gap between their ears with knowledge, ideas, ambitions, positive thoughts, and optimistic visions. Others clog up the gap with destructive negative thoughts, continually boosted by aggression, anger, frustration, envy, bitterness, or worry. Still others turn the gap into a fuzzy haze through illegal stimulants, which starts out as recreational use and ends up as reliance abuse. And a few, about 20 percent, introduce a spiritual element into the gap and find contentment. It is a contentment available only to those who acknowledge and understand the purpose of the space where earthly experience and spiritual enlightenment combine for the good of one and, ultimately, for the good of all.

The 10-Year Glitch

CHAPTER NINETEEN

Happy New Beginning

A decision to replace the sadness of ending with the exciting possibilities of a beginning is a liberating act for mind and body. The beginning of a new year is, for most people, a time of high expectation generated by a perceived (or hoped for) promise of bigger, brighter, better things to come. New Year's Eve is a universal celebration of a beginning and is one of the few occasions when the majority of the world's population unites in an unabashed display of positive anticipation.

There is no universal celebration for the ending of the old year. Ending represents the completion of a past involvement and therefore can no longer be accessible for change or influence. It is a **termination period** for personal growth.

Beginning a new year represents the chance for fresh achievement, development of skill and potential, and the chance to explore beyond comfort zones. It is a **continuation period** for personal growth.

Much of life's irritations, along with the anxiety, pain, and suffering endured by many people, are due to an unwillingness (or fear) to end an unsatisfactory element of their life. An emotion-draining relationship, a stress-inducing job, a deteriorating neighborhood, or any type of less-than-acceptable circumstance can all be overcome by courage-backed decisions to make a new beginning. The recurring question, *Can I start again?* and the unknown future factor associated with the question are the main reasons why many struggle to clear the way for a new beginning.

Of all the challenging recurring questions of life, it is perhaps one of the easier ones to tackle, because the valuable element of experience is there to help.

All effort that follows a decision for a new beginning is energy promoting, as opposed to the energy-sapping result of indecision and procrastination. These terrible twins are most responsible for the self-doubt that leads to a lack of action to end that which should be banished to the obsolete past.

A factor that plays a vital role in both beginning and ending, and is an essential element in preparing the mind for a new beginning, is the function of **memory.** The memory function provides the main thrust, influence, and direction in decision making. People are products of their pasts. What people are today is a direct result of their past thoughts and actions. What they will be in the future will be determined by what they retain from the past or change in the present.

Memory Stores and Recalls all!

In 10-Year Glitch terms, the fifth decade is a time for evaluation—a time for a mental clearout. Compare the process to the physical process of an annual spring cleaning. Apart from the thorough cleaning, it is also the time when attics, sheds, spare rooms, garages, and cupboards are cleared of items accepted as being no longer useful, necessary, or **worthy of occupying valuable space.**

Happy New Beginning

A mental evaluation and subsequent clearing of memories no longer relevant, important, or worthy of occupying valuable space is an ideal and highly recommended step in preparing the mind for a new beginning. Although memories cannot be erased, a built-in memory process banishes unwanted memories to labyrinths not readily accessible to the conscious mind. The process will greedily accept negative-generating memories such as unwanted guilt or blame, past failures or mistakes, and any reason (so far) for not achieving goals, ambitions, desires, or dreams. An appreciation of the amazing versatility and potential of memory function can be gleaned from a comparison between three diverse subjects:

- *Traditional thinking*
- *Metaphysical understanding*
- *Development of the universe as theorized by the world's most advanced scientific minds*

Traditional thinking's explanation for memory function is presented as a three-stage process. In **stage one**, known as **registration**, information is received and understood. It is then retained in a short-term memory system that seems to be very limited in the amount of material it can store at one time. Unless refreshed by constant repetition, the contents of short-term memory are lost within minutes and replaced by other material. In **stage two**, if information is **important** enough, it may be transferred into the long-term memory, where the process of storage involves association with words or meanings, visual imagery, and other experiences such as smell or sound. **Stage three**, the final stage, is **recall** (or retrieval), in which information stored at an unconscious level is brought, at will, into the conscious mind. The reliability of recall depends on how well the material was coded at stage two.

The 10-Year Glitch

Traditional thinking is unsure about the mechanism for storing memory. One theory offered is that memory may be held in the chemical structure of some substance in brain cells, possibly spare DNA that is not being utilized to hold the genetic code. As with many mind functions, the traditional explanation is cautious and non-committal, yet adamant that any explanation outside or beyond current findings and theories is nothing more than fanciful imagining devoid of reality. In the case of memory, traditional thinking insists that *memory function begins and ends within a life span.*

Traditional thinking's insistence on memory existing only within an earthly life span is a direct challenge to metaphysical understanding in a number of areas, specifically in the area known as **reincarnation**, the field that covers past-life theory. To appreciate the limited scope of traditional thinking and its inhibitive effect on alternative thinking, one need only study the stuttering unraveling of ideas on the origin of the Universe.

Up until the end of the nineteenth century, Sir Isaac Newton's concept of a Clockwork Universe was the accepted, final, and non-negotiable theory. Albert Einstein's General Theory of Relativity challenged Newton's laws and, in the 1920's, physicists developed the Quantum Theory that also caused a total re-think of what was once considered irrefutable knowledge. At the time, science did not really contemplate the idea of a beginning to the Universe, because the Universe was perceived as eternal and unchanging.

In 1969, the two most advanced minds in the scientific world, Professors Stephen Hawking and Roger Penrose, published their momentous theorems proving mathematically that the Universe must have been born out of a singularity some 15 billion years ago. Their Big Bang theory once again emphasized the folly of calling anything final and therefore impossible to be disputed or even questioned.

Happy New Beginning

For those on a spiritual path, the journey at times seems to be almost a New Frontier experience. As with the slow, painstaking efforts to discover the origin of the Universe, it will take the same dedication to overcome traditional thinking tardiness in order to participate in what could become the next great worldwide mainstream experience—*the acceptance and establishment of the New Age*. It is certain to happen, because there will always be people willing to promote new thoughts, new attitudes, new ideas, and new feelings, and to study them from all angles, because that is the way self-doubt becomes belief and new beginnings become a way of life.

At the forefront of all new beginnings will be memory, the most perfect function of all mind functions. As the metaphysical understandings become clearer, it may be revealed that memory exists before birth and continues after death. That, in turn, will provide a more credible explanation for such puzzles as déjà vu, French for *"already seen."*

The Oxford Dictionary states *"Déjà vu is an illusory feeling of having already experienced a present situation."* The use of the word *"illusory"* is a suitably vague explanation technique that allows traditional thinking to remain ensconced in a comfort zone.

The **metaphysical** understanding of reincarnation is a far more courageous explanation of déjà vu: *the rebirth of a soul in a new body*. When linked to the perpetuating memory theory, it provides a bridge to span the credibility chasm. It also answers the questions of whether it is possible to imagine something if it has not previously been physically experienced and whether child prodigies simply continue what their souls previously began at another time.

A new beginning is generally given life via the powerful character trait of optimism, and optimism has provided the launching pad of all achievement thus far evident in the Universe. One proven method for making and keeping a New

The 10-Year Glitch

Year resolution is the six-month step challenge. It starts with asking the following question: *within the next six months, what would you like…*

- *To overcome?*
- *To give up?*
- *To change?*
- *To learn?*
- *To obtain?*
- *To achieve?*

Most resolutions fail because people neglect to set a time limit for their challenge and the resolution is more general than specific.

Following are some of the answers given by participants attending a motivational self-growth seminar at which the six-month step challenge was used as part of the instruction material:

- *To overcome*…lack of motivation — worrying about what other people think — fear of confrontation — fear of future security
- *To give up*…leaving things until the last minute — being overly critical of others — smoking — chocolate — procrastination
- *To change*…the way my life is at the moment — judgmental attitude — my defeatist thinking during competitive sport
- *To learn*…assertiveness — new skills — relaxation
- *To obtain*…better relationships with my family — financial advice and direction

- *To achieve*...positive recognition of my talents — ways to have more fun in my social life

These answers demonstrate that resolutions based on purely material objectives often fail due to a weakness in the psychological makeup of the person making the resolution. In other words, he or she is not mentally ready to achieve the physical aspect of the resolution. The accuracy of that observation is contained in the saying *"When the mind is ready, all is ready."*

Another aspect of the New Year resolution theme could be called *"Out with the old, in with renew."*

It seems an ever-increasing number of people take an almost perverse delight in breaking their resolution within days or weeks of the New Year getting started. Those who claim they no longer bother making a New Year resolution because they feel disappointed when they break them further undermine the resolution tradition. Unfortunately, the breaking of a resolution often means a return to living out the year ahead buffeted by circumstances and existing within the rigid framework of unwanted habits.

If the New Year resolution tradition is losing (or has completely lost) its influence, then the time could be right to replace it with something that will rekindle what, in theory, is an essential element in obtaining quality of life during the earthly existence. For many people, the annual New Year resolution ritual is the only time they:

- *Set a goal.*
- *Decide on a change of direction.*

The 10-Year Glitch

- *Attempt to motivate themselves to start or complete a long-cherished project. Very few things in life can match the satisfaction of achieving something you have desired to achieve, or achieving something others said you could not achieve.*

It is also the perfect time to examine the 10-Year Glitch cycle and deal with any recurring questions affecting that particular decade's harmonious and successful progress. The following recurring questions are usually the ones that can benefit from a New Year analysis and resolution:

- *Am I where I should be?*
- *When should I say it is over?*
- *Can I start again?*

Remember…failing to deal with recurring questions can lead to difficulty in dealing with the recurring question, *Should I fear the future?*

One reason for the New Year resolution losing its impact and life-enhancing value is that something old exerting a far stronger mental influence often hinders achieving something new.

Most people will experience the mental aberration responsible for the condition at some time during a life span. This insidious, sinister, debilitating, mind-confusing condition is called **regret**.

The definition of regret reveals its potential for causing ongoing harm to both mind and body. Definitions include:

- *Being sorry for loss*
- *Wishing one could have again*
- *Being distressed about or sorry for an event or fact*
- *Grieving or repenting for an action*

Regret is an underrated yet highly damaging mental condition. This condition can be obvious, but it can also be lodged surreptitiously in the mind, creating havoc to health and happiness. It is a condition that can start from a single, seemingly innocent event but can then quickly gather strength from other negative sources which, when combined, soon create a major crisis.

This condition can be both self-induced and created sometimes unwittingly, sometimes deliberately, by friends, relatives, or partners. Symptoms and side effects of the regret condition include:

- *Anger*
- *Frustration*
- *Loss of self-esteem*
- *Stress-related mental conditions, such as anxiety, fear, and a general feeling of loss of control*

Guilt and **blame** are natural allies of regret. A New Year **regret elimination** would prove an ideal replacement or alternative to the New Year resolution. An unresolved regret is no different from an unhealed, open wound. It is painful, irritating, and provides a constant reminder of the cause. The mental burden of a major regret can lead to a mind-numbing condition that slowly but surely becomes depression. Adopting the **regret-elimination technique** harnesses the power of autosuggestion, the same motivating element that makes the New Year resolution so successful when persistence and determination are added to the mix.

The element of suggestion is used to activate and sustain the Gypsy, Egyptian, and voodoo types of curse, and many case histories exist demonstrating the power of dire warnings on those receiving them. However, little, if anything, is mentioned about the Western society curse capable of proving just as devastating as any ancient fulmination: *"If you do that, you'll regret it for the rest of your life!"*

It is usually uttered to young, receptive minds by all manner of well-meaning adults and can be an admonishment for any number of perceived misdemeanors. That one irresponsible utterance can plant the germ of guilt, and ultimately regret, which can last a lifetime, especially if the admonishment was for something of a sexual nature.

The following case history examples illustrate how regret, or guilt, or blame, can progress from an innocuous beginning to a complex ending.

"I am a parent who was so career-conscious I was too busy to spend quality time with my children during their developmental years. Now, when I try to make up for my supposed lack of caring, they reject my efforts and good intentions. I accept the blame and feel guilty, but it's the regret of not being able to retrieve the situation that causes me the most heartache."

"I am a young adult who blames my parents for my drug abuse problem. I don't speak to them or try to get in touch with them. Every now and then, I really regret the situation, but I just don't know how to change it."

"My sister and I didn't speak to each other for twenty years following a family squabble. My sister died suddenly a year ago.

Happy New Beginning

I wanted to end the feud many times, but now I greatly regret I won't get the chance to say I'm sorry."

Death, of course, reveals many hidden, forgotten, or ignored regrets. Death takes away the chance to repair, change, talk over, or otherwise eliminate regret. Unless one believes in life after death, reincarnation, or some other form of psychic phenomenon, all forms of communication cease with the deceased, but the regret can live on with those left behind.

During a Personality Evaluation test, participants were asked this confrontational question: *"What absolute truth would you like to state in your dying moments?"* Maximum points were given for the answer *"I have no regrets."*

Further questions and answers on the topic of regret revealed how easy it is for them to develop into major, life-debilitating problems if not corrected or eliminated during their embryo stages. In addition, minor regrets can be firmly established in the mind but not acknowledged as having any influence on behavior. However, oft-repeated statements can indicate latent regrets.

1. *"I had the talent, and I should have done something about it, but now it's too late."*
2. *"I was happy where I was, but I got talked into moving."*
3. *"I hate my job, but the money I earn is good."*
4. *"I knew at the time it was the wrong thing to do, but life goes on, so I've just got to try to forget it happened."*

Each of the above could be corrected by a 10-Year Glitch evaluation, along with a courageous and honest application of several recurring questions of life. They can also be applied to any one of the three stages of regret:

- *Haunted by a regret from the past*
- *Anxious about a regret existing in a present situation*
- *Worried about a regret arising from a decision to be made about the future*

Health represents a major proportion of the regret condition, and it is directly affected by a self-induced regret that has spawned a personality type known as a **regret masochist**. To identify this personality type, listen for apologetic statements such as, *"I really shouldn't"* just before they:

- *Smoke a cigarette when their throat is red and raw from a heavy cold*
- *Drink red wine knowing they have a histamine-intolerance*
- *Eat something they know will viciously upset their digestive system before causing a splitting headache*

A serious side to regret masochism is the possibility of it ultimately leading to hearing doom-laden statements such as, *"You should have thought about that before it got this far!"* or from the grim surgeon, *"I'm afraid it's too late for us to do anything for you."*

A guaranteed way to build up a stockpile of regrets, both minor and major, is to live a life directed or manipulated by other people when doing so creates a constant source of irritation, tension, frustration, or suppressed anger.

Happy New Beginning

The New Year regret eliminator, along with the 10-Year Glitch analysis and the recurring questions of life application, is the perfect technique for curbing the onslaught of regret before it reaches epic proportions. Applying the technique is as easy as identifying the regret or, if there are more than one, making a list of any regrets that cause discomfort when thought about. At the same time, list any current endeavors or situations that could lead to a future regret if something is not done **immediately** to avoid or stop the regret escalation.

If a major regret exists, be determined to develop the courage to confront and eliminate it for the sake of your health and future quality of life. If you decide that elimination is impossible at this time, develop the wisdom to accept that if the cause cannot be eliminated, you can change the effect by not allowing it to dominate your thoughts.

The less regret dominates, the weaker it gets, and the sooner it loses its influence.

For any and all other regrets existing at the beginning of a new year, ask this question: *"If I don't eliminate the regret now, will it be a bigger regret this time next year?"*

The 10-Year Glitch

CHAPTER TWENTY

It is All in the Mind

How important is the mind in most things pertaining to surviving the journey through life? Following are a number of well-known sayings, all with the mind as the focal point. Fill in the blank spaces to complete the sayings. Answers are on the following page.

1. It's _____ _____ the mind.
2. It's just a case of _____ over _____.
3. I'm sorry, but I've _____ _____ my mind.
4. What the mind of a person can conceive and _____, it can achieve.
5. Please _____ up your mind.
6. When the mind is ready, _____ things are ready.

Mind over Medicine

"It's all in the mind" is the expression many traditional medical practitioners use when their drugs and expertise fail to cure a patient's physical problems. The irony associated with the statement is that many of the physical body's problems can be traced to the mind and its myriad **thoughts.** For many years, people suffering from Chronic Fatigue Syndrome or Attention Deficit Disorder were dismissed as malingerers or hypochondriacs. Today, slowly but surely, an increasing number of forward-looking doctors are open to a fresh approach and are no longer **pigeonholing** patients via medical textbooks.

A major difference between alternative therapies and traditional medical procedures is the language used to describe ailments and cures. Complementary health practitioners talk about inner child work, mind/body energy blocks, and nutrition as opposed to conventional medical terms such as exploratory examination, surgical procedure, and drugs. When taking their first tentative steps outside the area of conventional medical treatment, most people discover the wide scope and variety of complementary healing therapies when attending an Alternative Lifestyle Exposition.

The steady growth of this type of public awareness outlet is either testament to the increasing success of complementary healing therapies or to a growing disillusionment in drug- and surgery-oriented traditional medical treatment. Walking into a massive exhibition center for the first time and seeing it full of complementary healing practitioners is a mind-boggling experience for any person who thought health care was the exclusive domain of traditional medical practitioners.

Within a few hours, newcomers will have added extensively to their vocabulary, including words and expressions such as reflexology, therapeutic massage, aura light analysis, acupuncture, and naturopathy. These are but a few of the

It is All in the Mind

many complementary healing modalities currently available as **alternatives** (not substitutes) to traditional medical procedures.

Sir William Osler, the first professor of medicine at the world-famous Johns Hopkins University School of Medicine, indicated future thinking of Western medicine when he said

> *"While we doctors often overlook or are ignorant of our own faith cures, we are just a wee bit too sensitive about those performed outside our ranks. Faith in the Saints cures one while faith in a pill cures another. Hypnotic suggestion cures a third while faith in a medical doctor cures a fourth. The faith with which we work is a most precious commodity without which we would be badly off."*

"Outside our ranks" is, of course, a strong reference to Eastern medical philosophies and complementary healing methods, most of which have their origins in Eastern medical practices.

While Western medicine continues to concentrate on treating the disease, Eastern healing methods continue to concentrate on treating the cause in the belief that healing is, in many instances, very much a matter of *"mind over medicine."*

Answers to "mind" quiz:

1 – It's **all in** the mind.

2 – It's just a case of **mind** over **matter.**

3 – I'm sorry, but I've **made up** my mind.

4 – What the mind of a person can conceive and **believe**, it can achieve.

5 – Please **make** up your mind.

6 – When the mind is ready, **all** things are ready.

Healthy Mind—Healthy Body

At a recent personal growth seminar, participants were given three minutes to compile a list of twenty or more ways to exercise the body. The target number was quickly and easily surpassed within the time span and ranged from walking and swimming to jogging and cycling, with pumping iron acknowledged as one of the more aggressive and strenuous ways to exercise.

Following a discussion about the mind-body relationship, the participants agreed that a healthy mind is an essential adjunct for a healthy body. They were then asked, in the same time span, to compile a list of ways to exercise the mind.

Before reading on, compile your own list of mind exercises…

Apart from the dubious candidates of wrestling with a weighty problem and jumping to conclusions, the participants found the task far harder than its physical counterpart. Millions of dollars, and hundreds of hours, are spent on keeping the body fit and healthy in order to fulfill the maxim *"You are what you train."* A similar effort is expended in pursuit of proving the axiom *"You are what you eat."* Although neither has anywhere near the same health impact or significance of *"You are what you think,"* very little time or money goes toward weight-reduction programs for fatheads!

It is All in the Mind

A perfect example of a healthy, vibrant mind sustaining a less-than-perfect physical being is evident in the mind and body of the brilliant scientist, Professor Stephen Hawking. At age twenty-one, Professor Hawking contracted the muscle-wasting disease known as Motor Neurone and was given two-and-a-half years to live. Although the disease caused his once healthy **body** to become so twisted and paralyzed as to affect most physical functions, at age fifty-one (thirty years after the death sentence), he was acclaimed as the greatest living scientist with possibly the world's finest **mind!** "When the mind is ready, all things are ready" is certainly a highly applicable truth in the case of Professor Hawking, as well as many others who have overcome physical limitations because of their fit, healthy, positive minds.

Exercise requires the three essentials of action, movement, and effort to obtain desired results. When it comes to exercising the mind, however, the three essentials often become a physical health hazard for many people. Exercising the mind with worry (of all kinds), anxiety, fear, frustration, envy, jealousy, anger, brooding, guilt, excessive grieving, and depression all provide action, movement, and effort, but they also cause short- and long-term damage to a healthy body.

The physical equivalent of such useless endeavor would be riding a pushbike with oblong wheels, swimming up the face of a waterfall, jogging on quicksand, aerobic sessions to the beat of a funeral march, or weightlifting with feathers…pumping irony!

Research programs conducted in the field of neuro-psychology, the study of the relationship between the nervous system, especially the brain, and behavior so far has discovered up to four hundred complex chemical substances secreted in the brain. Most of them are health promoting and, in normal, balanced functioning conditions, travel throughout the body servicing the immune and nervous system, as well as organs, cells, and glands. Negative emotions, as listed above, upset the orderly chemical distribution, whereas influences such as positive mental exercises not only maintain the harmonious balance, they also prevent the flow of the not-so-good chemicals. Excessive or prolonged use of any kind of stimulants or man-made drugs will cause **confusion** in the **distribution procedure** and a subsequent breakdown of the mind-to-body health and healing process.

What Are Ideal Mental Exercises?

Chess, board games, crossword puzzles, and a variety of computer applications all provide the mind with healthy exercise via stimulation, but they can also limit its scope and development if not combined with at least some of the following:

- *Memory exercises* help to repair the irresponsible damage caused by people saying they have a hopeless memory because they cannot remember names, telephone numbers, appointments, and so on; and yet, those same hopeless memories that cannot remember a name given five minutes previously can recall an unlimited number of lifetime memories!

  Repeatedly commenting about a bad memory function is an affirmation, and an affirmation is one of the most powerful sources for influencing the mind. Does anyone use the other methods for influencing the mind as a way to develop a poor memory? Would they pray, visualize, imagine, or ardently desire to develop a bad memory?

  The memory is one of the most perfect functions of the human condition and simply needs a regular maintenance program to keep it at peak performance. Diaries, planners, and writing notes are the best methods of exercising the memory, because it thrives on receiving unlimited information (good or bad), and it can be conditioned into a habit of remembering anything and everything it has received and is required to act upon!

- *Curiosity* is a mental exercise. In extensive studies carried out by neurobiologists, results strongly indicate that a mind continually challenged with new information will remain vigorous, creative, and healthy into old age.

- *Flexible thinking* is a mental exercise. A closed mind becomes stagnant in the same manner that a clear water pond becomes stagnant if fresh water no longer flows into it.

- *Meditation* is a mental exercise. It provides a means for stopping a tumble dryer mind, in which a host of negative thoughts churn endlessly in a haphazard cycle, resulting in a destructive waste of valuable mental energy. Meditation opens the door of the machine so that we can take out the washing.

- *Enthusiasm* is a priceless mental exercise. It provides the ignition factor that keeps various parts of the mind firing at their optimum level.

- *Positive thinking* is the supreme mental exercise. It can be likened to fresh, crystal-clear spring water swishing in and out of the mind's labyrinth, washing away the pollution, scum, and decay caused by negative thoughts and thinking.

The 10-Year Glitch

This is a good spot in which to comment on the way positive thinking is often maligned by people who consider it a Pollyanna or unrealistic approach to life in general. The truth is that anything worthwhile requires effort to obtain and retain. An optimistic, positive-thinking attitude takes effort to develop, but once established, it requires constant vigilance to offset pessimistic and negative influences from people and circumstances. A pessimistic, negative attitude requires absolutely no effort whatsoever to develop and sustain. A study of any of the truly great achievements throughout history reveals that it was optimism and positive thinking at the core of each achievement.

An ideal way to sum up this section, and emphasize the importance of a healthy, positive mental attitude, is to say: *Think fit or think sick…your body demands and relies on the right choice!*

A Funny Mind

When a person says, *"I haven't laughed so much for years,"* they may have denied themselves a source of pain and stress relief supplied free of charge by his/her own body.

"Laughter is the best medicine," like many oft-quoted philosophies, is accepted for its inherent wisdom without its meaning being fully understood. Medical science texts reveal that **endorphins** are the reason why a bout of laughter can lift your spirits and make you feel better for the experience.

Endorphins are a group of substances formed within the body that relieve pain. They have a similar chemical structure to morphine and act at specific sites (called opiate receptors) in the brain, spinal cord, and other nerve endings. In addition to their analgesic effect, endorphins are thought to be involved in controlling the body's response to stress and determining mood.

It is All in the Mind

In clinical psychology studies, it has been found that people with a healthy sense of humor have fewer emotional problems than those who find it difficult to laugh, particularly at themselves. As the mind and body thrive on **established habits**, a laughter habit would obviously be a way to benefit from laughter as medicine. Movies, television, videos, and books are the easiest method for creating a regular laughter habit and are a guaranteed way to keep the endorphins active and life enhancing. Conversely, it is important not to make grief, bad times, or unfortunate circumstances an excuse to avoid or stop laughter for too long, because laughter can shorten the low times and hasten the passing of any detrimental situation.

The late Michael Bentine, a man who throughout his lifetime of comedy and humor performances on stage, radio, and television, gave immense pleasure to millions of people, supplied a good example. Bentine lived by a simple but effective philosophy: *"You can either laugh or cry in life."*

This philosophy held him together through family tragedies more numerous than one person should bear. A journalist interviewing Bentine after yet another harrowing experience said of the encounter, *"I expected to feel sad after the interview, but I came away feeling happy, inspired, and special."*

A leading American heart specialist once said to a leading American comedian, *"A weekly visit to one of your shows would be as beneficial for some of my patients as a weekly visit to me."*

Whenever black, brooding thoughts darken your mood, tell yourself to lighten up and laugh, and keep repeating it until you do. It is a sure way to understand, appreciate, and benefit from the mind-healing tonic of laughter. Remember…a miserable-looking face does not happen by chance. It comes from thinking miserable thoughts!

The 10-Year Glitch

CHAPTER TWENTY-ONE

The Motivated Mind

In chapter nine, "It Is a Long Road that Has No Signposts," the subject of thoughts received by the mind was detailed. We now revisit that topic from another angle.

According to scientific research data, the average, normal mind receives thousands of thoughts during a twenty-four hour period. Naturally, the majority of the thoughts are categorized as fleeting, thus requiring minimum mind space due to their inconsequential nature.

The second category of thoughts are those associated with the current day's activities and can include what to eat, what to wear, where to go, what to do, who to see, and who to avoid. Most of the thoughts stem from established habits and are therefore easily absorbed into a daily routine with little fuss or bother.

It is the third category of thought that can lead to a mind condition best described as a **tumble dryer mind.** Picture a tumble dryer full of clothes. The clothes churn and tumble around in a haphazard fashion and will continue to do so until the cycle ends, the door is opened, or the dryer is turned off. If none of those three things happened, the dryer's motor would eventually **burn out**, leaving the clothes in a jumbled, useless pile. Relate that now to a host of negative thoughts churning and tumbling around in a haphazard fashion and continuing to do so until some mental action is taken to release the thoughts.

What mental state could result from not releasing the thoughts?

Picture now a crystal-clear pond with fresh, drinkable water flowing in from one side and ultimately, after reaching a certain level, flowing out from the opposite side, enabling the pond to retain its pure, healthy, flowing condition.

Destroying the pond's pure, life-enhancing attributes is simply a matter of blocking both the inward and outward flow. In a short time, the water remaining in the pond becomes the very opposite of pure and healthy, eventually reaching the health-destroying condition known as **stagnation**—motionless, having no current (when applied to the pond), and dull, sluggish, lacking positive activity (when applied to life, business, and **the mind**). When new, fresh, positive thoughts are prevented from entering the mind, and existing negative thoughts cannot exit, the comparison to the stagnant pond becomes a valid and easily understood example.

When a mind is full of negative thoughts churning around and around, they will continue to do so until the cycle is broken and the orderly flow of in-and-out thoughts is restored. Failure to achieve that aim can lead to mental burnout and ultimately **depression,** the mind's equivalent to stagnation.

The following list details the main causes of the tumble dryer mind condition.

Worry is the most common and prevalent cause for the condition.

If one of the recurring questions of life had been *"must I worry?"*, the answer would be an emphatic *no!* Constant and continuous worry is pure poison to the mind and serves absolutely no useful or productive purpose. Never let the mind be clogged with the insidious malady of worry.

Fear in any of its many forms is a guaranteed way to create the tumble dryer mind condition.

As a positive attribute, fear sharpens the senses, gives extra strength, and quickens reactions, all of which help to respond to a threatening or dangerous situation. These attributes create fearless heroes—usually fearless only for the duration of a particularly demanding episode in their lives.

As a negative attribute, however, fear can cause the tumble dryer mind aberration to develop when the fear does not seem to have an obvious cause, is excessive for the circumstances, or continues long after the initial cause of the fear. Any of the three can allow fear to become a way of life, making fear itself the true problem, hence the truth in the expression, *"There's nothing to fear but fear itself."*

An interesting and motivational aspect of fear is contained in the following observations:

- *Have you ever had doubts about your capacity to cope?*
- *When you are trying to do something new, or solve an important problem, do you experience or suffer from disconcerting physiological symptoms such as sweating, increased tension, rapid pulse rate, or a churning stomach?*

- *Do you worry that you may not have what it takes to deal with the situation?*
- *If you answer yes, then relax, because you are experiencing a normal reaction!*
- *Such symptoms and obstacles are common manifestations of anxiety and occur regularly with most people.*
- *Achiever types may experience even more of the discomforts than others may because they take on more challenges and face the recurring questions of life more often. However, they are also able to ignore their anxiety and focus their energy on getting the job done.*
- *Though they may be fearful prior to tackling the challenge, they do not resort to a stimulant boost to reduce the fear. Instead, they use their anxiety for the initial thrust of action!*
- *Fear is the single strongest motivating force in our lives, so whatever you do, do not try to calm your fears. Acknowledge them, accept them as normal, and do whatever has to be done.*

Complexes are unconscious or conscious perceptions of some abnormal condition that at any time can dominate the thought process and cause a destructive tumble dryer mind cycle. The complex can stem from ideas, beliefs, or memories with great emotional importance or significance.

Grieving, especially when regret or guilt is a major contributor to the grieving process.

Unresolved emotions, including all the health-debilitating mind conditions such as anger, resentment, envy, jealousy, and frustration. A potent secret involving self or another will also ultimately lead to a tumble dryer mind condition because the longer a secret is kept, the more damaging the repercussions when it is finally revealed.

Procrastination, especially if something of extreme importance needs to be done but is continually avoided, thus allowing it to increase steadily in importance to the point of adversely affecting the mind's healthy function.

One example of that situation stems from the making of a last will and testament. A person in their 20s or 30s may not attach much importance to drawing up a will, and he/she probably will not be adversely affected by not doing so. However, from the 50's and 60's on, the importance of making out a will increases each year. Procrastination will exert constant mental pressure until the task is tackled and completed.

The following list provides ways to avoid or overcome the tumble dryer mind condition;

Five-star Mind

A five-star hotel achieves that status due to seeming perfection in every facet of its operation. From the greeting and attentive service upon entering the premises to the beautifully appointed room and from the superb restaurant meals to the many facilities available, all have the aim of making life within the hotel a memorable, stress-free experience.

Everything you **see** and experience represents five-star qualities, but what about the things you do not see or experience? For example, does the kitchen operate completely free of accidents or of things going wrong? Of course not, but the mishap or any problem will be fixed as soon as practically possible, and the guests will rarely, if ever, know about it.

What if one or more of the staff is feeling off-color or battling a personal emotional crisis not associated with his/

her workplace? Again, the guests will never know because each member of the staff is trained to present a positive, enthusiastic, friendly face and manner regardless of his/her personal feelings at the time.

And so it is with everything in a five-star establishment—any problems, irritations, mishaps, accidents, or disruptive influences are dealt with as quickly as possible in order to return the establishment to its orderly and efficient operation, thus providing a seemingly perfect environment for the guests. Compare that with a one- or two-star hotel. Problems, irritations, mishaps, accidents, or disruptive influences are dealt with—eventually!

Now, compare the working of the mind with the foregoing examples. It is possible and is a goal worth striving for, to achieve a **five-star mind**, in which negative or disruptive thoughts are dealt with *as soon as practically possible* with the aim of returning the mind to its orderly and efficient function. Using one or more of the following techniques will help to achieve the goal:

Confront and Eliminate

The tumble dryer mind condition begins with, and it is sustained by, **not** confronting the negative, destructive thoughts causing the condition. Ideally, the moment a tumble dryer mind condition is apparent, the thought(s) causing the condition should be **identified** and **confronted**, and immediate steps should be taken to **eliminate** the thought(s).

Ignoring the thoughts, or hoping they will go away of their own volition, is akin to allowing a physical medical condition to get worse steadily by ignoring it or hoping it will go away without receiving urgent attention. Using this technique is not easy or palatable and is often thwarted by excuses, but for short- and long-term peace of mind and quality of life, it has to be accomplished one way or another.

Flow Through

If it is not possible to confront and eliminate negative, destructive thoughts immediately, then the **flow through technique** can act as a temporary solution, a way of turning off the power until the confront-and-eliminate procedure can be applied. As soon as destructive thoughts are identified as being capable of creating a tumble dryer mind condition, it is vital that the thoughts enter and exit in a **flow through pattern** and not be allowed to dwell long enough to influence the mind's positive thought process. Thinking or quietly saying *"flow through"* whenever the negative, destructive thoughts enter the head and repeating it until the thoughts exit, allows the mind time and space to become strong enough to prepare for the confront and eliminate stage.

Top-class sports people all use the powerful and potent **flow through technique** in the heat of competition, where negative and destructive thoughts will severely lessen their ability to compete and win. It is an especially valuable aid whenever an important event is looming and self-doubt tries to infiltrate and start a tumble dryer mind cycle.

Thought Substitution

As mentioned in an earlier chapter, the physical body cannot react to two thoughts at the same time. The body can react to yes or no, I can or I cannot, I will or I will not, but *it cannot react to both at the same time. This is the motivational law that makes humans responsible for any and all of their actions!*

Similar to the flow through technique, it provides an instant result but requires a more imaginative approach. As soon as the negative, destructive thought enters the head, it should be immediately replaced with a positive, constructive substitution. The process is repeated each time the negative, destructive thought battles for headspace. As with the flow through technique, substituting positive for negative allows the mind time and space to become strong enough to prepare for the above confront and eliminate stage.

Meditation

Without a doubt, **meditation** provides a perfect environment for achieving the forgoing mind states as well as being a wonderful way to enjoy chosen periods of mental peace and harmony. It is also the ultimate example of the one-thought mind in action.

Meditation has been used to obtain spiritual enlightenment in many Eastern cultures for thousands of years, but to this day, it is still treated as an unknown quantity by the majority of Western mainstream society. The main reason for this attitude is that quality meditation requires concentration, persistence, and time, three enemies of Western society's fast-paced, flat-out busy, and time-selfish lifestyle.

One exciting development is the increasing interest and respect the healing power of meditation is gaining from sections of the medical profession. In numerous cases of health improvement and enhancement via meditation sessions rather than tranquilizer-type drugs, it is becoming apparent that drugs, as a first and often only treatment, are no longer the priority option.

Current research into the powerful health possibilities of meditation indicates short- and long-term benefits to breathing, brain activity, blood pressure, and pulse rate. The calm and rested feeling meditation produces should not only ease disorders of the moment but also improve the ability to cope physically and mentally with forthcoming activities or future problems. Quality meditation also provides a reliable, non-stimulant answer to the question posed by Saint Augustine: *"Where do I go to escape from me?"*

CHAPTER TWENTY-TWO

Moods and Emotions

One of the more mental and physical health-enhancing elements of life is the ability to control **mood** and **emotional swings.** In what appears to be an increasingly aggressive world, it is important for any number of reasons to find the balance between **assertive** and **aggressive** characteristics and behavior.

- *Aggressive people step over the line and invade other people's personal space.*
- *Assertive people stand their ground and do not invade.*

Aggressive people thrive on conflict. Therefore, their natural weakness will be the lack of retaliatory conflict. You cannot fight if there is no one to fight! They also hold the view that arguing is a positive attribute when, in fact, it is probably the least desirable or intelligent element in any communication between people.

Aggressive behavior is often used to **camouflage** a number of aberrations that include

The 10-Year Glitch

- *Unhappiness*
- *Frustration*
- *Insecurity*
- *Low self-esteem*
- *Health problems*

The **true essence** of assertiveness is the ability to express your right to be treated with respect as an intelligent, equal human being, able to interact with others without being dependent upon their approval. One advantage of achieving the true essence is that it enables a person to believe firmly they can and should say no without feeling guilty, unhappy, or anxious about the outcome. Understanding and adopting the ideals suggested in the mood and emotional swing indicator will prove a major step in overcoming aggressive behavior or developing and maintaining an assertive nature.

The following illustration uses the swing of a pendulum as a visual aid for explaining how controlling emotions can lead to many mental and physical benefits. The pendulum is used because of its precise and repeating swing to points exactly opposite to each other.

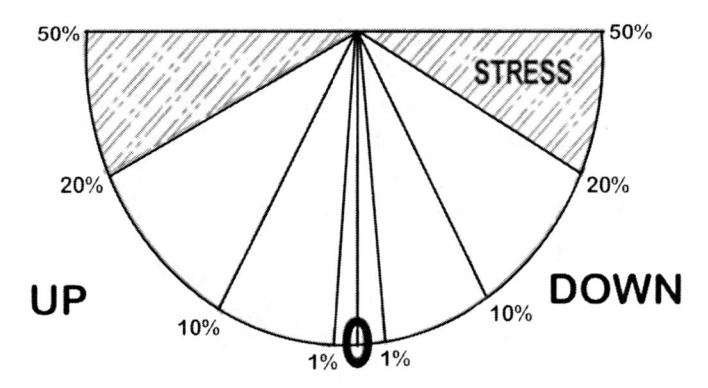

Moods and Emotions

Mood swings and changes are part of the healthy cyclic nature of the mind's function. The universe, via nature, demands **balance** in almost every aspect of earthly existence. In the human example, history shows that many extraordinarily gifted people invariably had an undesirable element in their life acting as a counterbalance to the talent or ability they had been given.

The average, stable person's moods and emotions remain balanced and evenly spread over long periods. The moody (and sometimes unstable) person's emotions vary in short bursts, to the point where relatives, friends, or associates are never sure what mood they will be confronted with at any given time.

The theory offered by the indicator suggests that a 20-20 mood swing is perfect for a balanced and healthy variation in mood and emotion. The practical application recommends that a mood swing never go beyond 20 percent in the UP side, thus preventing a detrimental swing beyond 20 percent in the DOWN side. Mood swings beyond the 20 percent mark place the mood and emotions into a **possible stress area** in the UP side and a **definite stress area** in the DOWN side.

The 1-1 swing is considered too timid for this modern world, although there is a section of society that can exist with an almost indiscernible 1 percent to 1 percent mood and emotional swing. The stress-free life in a monastery or convent enables monks and nuns to maintain a low mood and emotional swing because it is free of the hundred and one problems associated with *"life on the outside,"* most of which can cause regular doses of stress.

The 10-10 swing is perhaps too placid for a modern world, in which the pace of life is so fast and furious that surviving the hustle and bustle requires more than a meek and mild-mannered nature. Unfortunately, good manners and basic etiquette—two attributes compatible with a balanced swing—are currently struggling for a place in the scheme of things.

The 20-20 mood and emotional swing is an ideal figure because it allows scope to be as assertive as any given UP incident demands. Once completed, however, the natural swing back to the DOWN side is more of a cooling off, settling down, or relaxation period, rather than a time of questioning the need for the assertive action.

Between the 20% and 50% levels is the area in which blood pressure rises, along with a number of other physiological upheavals, during particularly assertive, important, or nerve-racking UP events. Building up events such as interviews, public speaking, new jobs, or any new challenge as the biggest and most important event ever will push the pendulum to unrealistic levels in the UP side. In addition, if things do not work out as imagined or anticipated, the disappointment will cause the swing to go way beyond healthy in the DOWN side. The term **anti-climax** is a clue to such a phenomenon.

Knowing and being aware of the kind of irritations and aberrations that cause unhealthy mood and emotional swings is one way of defeating their destructive influence.

Anger in its uncontrolled state, for any reason and under any circumstance, will guarantee a mood and an emotional swing beyond the safety zone. Anger in its controlled state is certainly a motivating force, able to be used in correcting a wrong or starting a necessary offensive action. The key, of course, is to have a clear mental picture of the mood and emotional swing indicator and to keep the anger level within the 20-20 range.

It is interesting to note that defense lawyers in court cases will set out to create anger and increase the mood and emotion swing of a witness by questioning the honesty, or accuracy, of their testimony. Lie detector tests tap directly into the mood and emotional swing factor for their results. Again, it is the anger or detection element stemming from the questions asked

Moods and Emotions

that send the pendulum swinging from UP stress to DOWN stress if the person being tested is telling lies.

Resentment and its close allies, **envy and jealousy**, can cause long-term destructive mood and emotional swings. Each time the cause of the aberrations is thought about, the pendulum will swing to its full width, causing any one of a number of physical ailments.

Frustration, especially if it is the result of **procrastination**, is a common cause for excessive mood and emotional swings. Not dealing with the recurring questions of life as soon as they are posed is a major cause of frustration.

Relatives and family relationships with antagonistic tendencies will cause unhealthy fluctuations, particularly on special occasions when family members should be on their best behavior but instead use the occasion to increase the antagonism.

Anxiety about major elements of life not always under personal control can lead to bouts of unhealthy mood and emotional swings. Health of self or someone close, other people's behavior, the way society is going, and fear of the future are some of the items included in this category.

Instant rage is an increasing and modern cause of serious mood and emotional swings. Although it is a form of anger, it does not belong in the anger section due to its instantaneous and often short-lived reaction.

Road rage is the best known of the instant rages, but many others are appearing due to a lack of tolerance, caring, feeling, and other interactions between people. The rapidly decreasing opportunity to communicate on a face-to-face basis, thanks to the rapid increase of technology, also plays a part.

Stimulant usage. Although this subject deserves more space, it is so well documented in all forms of the media on a

The 10-Year Glitch

daily basis that nothing new would be added here. It is simply well to know and acknowledge that stimulant use, regardless of the reason, is a major cause for constantly occurring, unhealthy mood and emotional swings.

CHAPTER TWENTY-THREE

The Mind and Memory

People are products of their pasts. What they are today has been shaped by past habits and patterns of behavior such as diet, relationships, events, physical actions, and the quality of thought and thinking. The amazing mind function called **memory** retains and stores all the foregoing personal data and releases portions of it as and when required by conscious request.

Unfortunately, memory also releases past personal data without conscious permission and will continue to do so unless a workable technique is used to control and release only what is useful, beneficial, and free of detrimental elements.

Whenever a person decides on any course of action with future success as its aim, past memory data will greatly influence the decision making. Past successes in a similar action means the memories released will be positive and beneficial, especially if confronted with recurring questions of life such as:

- *Am I where I should be?*
- *Can I start again?*
- *What if I get it wrong?*

Conversely, past failures will release negative memories and make decision making regarding the recurring questions a more challenging and courageous proposition. The very definition of decision—*a conclusion or resolution reached, especially as to future action*—indicates how important good, positive past memories can be in dealing with the recurring question of life, *Should I fear the future?*

One constant aspect greatly influencing the quality of life, the 10-Year Glitch, and the recurring questions of life is the battle between **thoughts that help** and **thoughts that hinder.**

Memory is the source for both help and hinder thoughts. Therefore, if memories that are no longer **relevant, applicable,** or **important** could be screened and then filtered before they exert influence on decision making, the task of present and future planning would become considerably less complicated or fearful.

Conditioning thoughts and thinking to **present-future** rather than **present-past** helps to create new, fresh, positive memories six months, nine months, twelve months, and years ahead. Any of the techniques for dealing with a tumble dryer mind condition, detailed in chapter twenty-one, will help in the screening and filtering process. As with any exercise, physical or mental, the more it is practiced, the more beneficial and easier it is to perform.

The recurring questions of life: *Can I start again?* and *What if I get it wrong?* provide perfect examples of the value obtained from applying the memory screening and filter process.

The need to ask, *Can I start again?* indicates something is no longer working and is no longer compatible or worthy of committing any further time, effort or caring attention.

Asking, *What if I get it wrong?* as a follow-up indicates a fear of repeating the actions that led to the current recurring question situation.

It can also suggest that there are too many negative memories interfering with what should be a fresh, positive approach.

A fear of the unknown is sometimes nothing more than a fear stemming from something that happened in similar previous circumstances. As mentioned earlier, if past challenges have been successful, any new challenge with similar characteristics will not present a problem in dealing with the recurring questions. The memories will be success-oriented and, therefore, both helpful and positive.

Conversely, if past challenges have had failure elements, the recurring questions will not be so easy to answer. Due to the memories being failure-oriented, they are hindering and negative. In that situation, screening and filtering memories is not only an essential factor for a successful outcome, it is also a safeguard against developing even more negative memories in the present that will be hindering memories in months and years ahead!

Important Decisions and Courses of Action

The biggest and most common fears when having to make an important decision or choosing a course of action are the fear of making a mistake and the fear of the unknown. Major factors in the process are the often-opposing forces of **logic versus emotion**, often referred to as **the head versus the heart**. A look at several of the recurring questions of life emphasizes just how difficult it can be to answer them with positive action if logic is pulling in the opposite direction from emotion.

- *Am I where I should be?*
- *When should I say it is over?*
- *Can I start again?*
- *What if I get it wrong?*

A reliable and proven technique for helping to overcome fears that cause bouts of indecision is a simple method known as

The For and Against Analysis

A sheet of paper is divided into two sections by drawing a line down the center. The left-hand side becomes the **for** list; the right-hand side, the **against** list. This technique enables both logic and emotion to contribute, with the idea being to complete the lists as quickly as possible, without thinking too hard or deeply. Just let the items flow to one side or the other. When the list items are exhausted (meaning when the **conscious mind** cannot add additional items**),** put the paper away for twenty-four hours and forget about it!

Not allowing any more thought on the matter is a vital and essential element in the success of the technique. During the twenty-four hour period, the sub-conscious will continue to work on the matter. The difference is that it will mix and match the logical and emotional elements and arrive at a compromise solution. People who understand the power of this technique refer to it as *taking a problem and sleeping on it.*

After twenty-four hours, the list is studied again. It is surprising how easy it is to add some new items to the lists or to remove items no longer valid or important enough to be on the lists.

If one list is far longer than the other is, it is a reliable indication for making a definite decision. If there are regrets about the decision at a later date (and it is rare), lack of careful thought cannot be used as a reason for the regret.

However, if the two lists are close, say within two or three items, most people will consider it inconclusive and therefore too risky to pursue a decision. In that case, each item on the two lists is given a rating number between one and twenty, based on their importance or significance. When all items have a number, add them together to see which list contains the highest number. Usually, there is a far bigger number gap between the lists, and the decision is clear.

If the gap is still too close for comfort, then stay put, because it is obviously not time for a successful decision. Attempting to force change will often backfire.

New Ventures and New Goals

The preceding technique is ideal whenever the chance to participate in a new venture or set new goals becomes an important factor for correcting an imbalance in one of the 10-Year Glitch decades or answering one of the recurring questions of life. It also provides a workable solution if life has become too **boring** and requires a fresh, new approach in order to add some much needed **joie de vivre**—*a feeling of healthy and exuberant enjoyment of life!*

New Partner Relationships

This is one area where memories of past relationships must be screened and filtered out as soon as possible. Nothing kills off a new partner relationship faster than talking about memories involving former partner(s). Comparing what a former partner did, or said, or was good at, or achieved, is an extremely insensitive way to treat a new partner, who is anticipating a fresh start not influenced by or reliant on past memories!

Second, Third, or Fourth Attempts

Many of the motivational teachings, suggestions, and advice contained within the pages of this book are aimed at correcting, changing, or overcoming something in **one attempt** in order to avoid drawn-out sagas that become increasingly more difficult to correct, change, or overcome if left unattended. However, it may sometimes take two, three, or even four (surely not more?) attempts before the ideal conclusion is reached. It is a situation that raises the question of how many times must a person keep trying before he/she hears the right answer, finds what he/she seeks, or achieves the blissful satisfaction of knowing he/she has discovered their personal paradise in the earthly existence.

If success in anything is proving elusive, the answer might be to look at **why** it is elusive rather than blindly trying repeatedly. Repeated failures often mean repeated habits not compatible with the hoped-for accomplishment. Again, the for and against analysis will almost certainly highlight the weakness causing the problem.

CHAPTER TWENTY-FOUR

Motivation in Action

The following poem was written anonymously many years ago. It has served as an inspiration for a wide variety of people who understand and acknowledge the power of the mind's influence in many of the aspects so far detailed within this book.

- *If you think you are beaten, you are; if you think you dare not, you don't;*
- *If you'd like to win, but think you can't, it's almost certain you won't.*
- *If you think you'll lose, you're lost, for out in the world we find*
- *Success begins with a person's will; it's all in the state of mind.*
- *Life's battles don't always go to the stronger or faster hand,*
- *But sooner or later the person who wins is the one who thinks I can!*

Many aspects of the earthly experience require knowledge of a formula in order to succeed and achieve in selected and desired endeavors. Two items briefly covered in earlier chapters are revisited here and used as perfect examples of **motivation in action**.

The tried and tested formula for succeeding in almost any desired endeavor states, *"Success happens when preparation meets opportunity."* The result of complying with the formula enables the **imagined self** to **bond** with the **actual self**. It is the wonderful time when what people have imagined themselves achieving sometime in the future eventually becomes the thing they have achieved in actuality. Success is always visible or apparent to the people with their sights set on achieving it.

Opportunity is also obvious and plentiful, because opportunity is one of the more abundant elements supplied by the universe. It is readily available to those who apply and follow the success formula to its conclusion.

There is often a set **preparation time** required in order to take advantage of future opportunities. A **passage of time** also runs parallel with the preparation time. Upon completion of the preparation time, the gap between imagining success and actual success closes, and the opportunity becomes a reality.

Achieving success is not always a clean-cut, start-to-finish endeavor. Many people achieve their success with **stop-start progress** and require a number of attempts before eventually achieving their imagined and actual bonding. Although failing on occasion, their belief in their actual self's ability to become their imagined self keeps them going until it becomes reality.

Obvious examples of the success formula in action are doctors, tradesmen, and professions such as law, accountancy, and engineering, to name just a few. Each example has a preparation time running parallel to the passage of time. A person intending to become a doctor must accept a five-year preparation time in order to fulfill the ambition and a further preparation period if the goal is to become a medical specialist. The trades and professions follow a similar pattern.

You are too late for the opportunity that is gone, but you are never too late for the opportunity that lies ahead.

That is good news to people such as writers, artists, musicians, actors, and entertainers, most of whom work on a freelance basis. *"Why don't you get a real job?"* is a barb most of them would have heard in their early days. However, the people with the real jobs would live in a very dull, culture-deficient world but for the courageous efforts of the freelance community, which forgoes job security in order to hone and polish their skills and talents. Their preparation and passage of time can be many years longer than the trades and professions and usually follows the stop-start route to success.

The **get-rich-quick path** to success is taken by people attempting to avoid any preparation time by going from nothing to success after accepting an opportunity that is *"too good to be true."* Going straight up, unfortunately, often ends in coming straight down with a crash.

A motivation challenge: The time to start taking positive action is today, and tomorrow, and every day thereafter, because action supplies the energy that turns a dream into reality!

Often, at the beginning of any decision to succeed at something, the gap between the imagined self and the actual self can seem so wide as to be almost impossible to close. A major reason for what appears to be a daunting prospect is the mistake of imagining the product (polished) the final step, instead of accepting the beginning product (rough) and taking the first step.

The following chart is a proven method for bridging the **imagined-actual gap** in an orderly, **10-step challenge**.

The 10-Year Glitch

		DATE	DATE
IMAGINED SELF	10 _____	_____	_____
	9 _____	_____	_____
	8 _____	_____	_____
	7 _____	_____	_____
	6 _____	_____	_____
	5 _____	_____	_____
	4 _____	_____	_____
	3 _____	_____	_____
	2 _____	_____	_____
	1 _____	_____	_____
ACTUAL SELF	0 _____	_____	_____

Imagined self (10) is the level that will provide the desired success factor. Whatever that is, it should be committed to writing in a succinct way on the line. The first date to the right of the line is the **anticipated date** for achieving the goal. The second date is the **actual date** of achieving the goal—a time for a major celebration upon the accomplishment of the challenge.

The six-month evaluation check— detailed in chapter nineteen—is ideal to kickstart the 10-step challenge.

Actual self (0) is the starting point. It is the time to evaluate self via the for and against analysis to make sure there is a realistic chance of achieving the goal. From that point, it is simply a matter of writing a mini goal and date on line one. Once the mini goal is achieved, the process continues **one line at a time** until number ten is reached and the major goal achieved.

Each mini goal should be a microcosm of the major goal, and each step should have some bearing on, or relationship with, the step ahead and the major goal.

Simple examples would include the weekly or monthly (mini goal) saving of a small sum of money toward the large sum of money required to achieve the major goal. When attempting to give up something that perhaps is detrimental to health and well-being, it is better to break down the major goal into smaller components. This allows a gentle, step-by-step approach rather than an all-out major goal assault that often collapses due to the magnitude of the challenge.

This technique is highly successful because it combines the potent and positive mind functions of determination, imagination, visualization, and persistence.

Although it can be a slow process initially, it does get faster when the law of attraction eventually takes hold as enthusiasm and belief increase with every mini-goal success.

This book evolved via a 10-step challenge!

Before proceeding with a challenge, it is important now to acknowledge and understand the following proven formula that accurately details the way people **retain information**.

Exhaustive tests on hundreds of subjects enabled researchers to establish the following data that has proven a boon to all who have accepted and absorbed its principle.

The 10% Theory

After finishing a non-fiction how-to book, *only 10% of the content is retained* following the first read-through. That information is usually surprising to people who are sure they have grasped most of the book's information in a first and only read-through. In addition, armed with this knowledge, people can appreciate why, after reading a how-to book once, they have not been able to achieve the success promised by the book's contents.

A good example of the theory in action is the number of times required to read and understand an instruction pamphlet or booklet accompanying an item requiring assembly. Rarely, if ever, can the task be accomplished with a single, often frustrating, read-through.

One ideal method for achieving maximum retention benefit from a non-fiction book is to highlight passages from the book that relate directly to a current situation. Then, highlight sections on second, third, and subsequent readings. It is surprising to discover that different sections are highlighted with each read-through, indicating that a personal development process is happening. What is vital, important, and highlighted during one particular reading is superseded by something else in a subsequent read-through.

Finally, throughout the chapters in this book, there are many suggestions and techniques aimed at achieving a harmonious and lasting quality of life. It may take a few reads to find the one that best suits your particular needs, or you may have already identified it. Either way, we wish you success in your personal growth development, regardless of which decade you are in.

Readers are encouraged to contact the authors via e-mail at margotandjohn@smartchat.net.au *or by mail directed in care of the Publisher.*

About the Authors

JOHN GALLAGHER

Born in London (England) but based in Australia (35 years) after residencies in Holland and New Zealand.

Freelance writing career at twenty eight years of age that includes television scriptwriter, magazine and advertising copy writing, and comedy sketch material for professional comedians on the Australian club and comedy circuit.

A lifelong interest in the mind's function and motivation eventually became a career opportunity as a Relationship Coach, leading to professional work via seminars, workshops and lecturing to a wide variety of people from all walks of life.

Author of two published novels: *The Golf Island Siege* and *The One Dollar Putt*.

The 10-Year Glitch

With co-author, Margot Maurice, published a personal growth and lifestyle magazine, and organised an annual New Age expo.

MARGOT MAURICE.

Born and living all her life in Australia, Margot's professional career in radio serials and children's programs started at the tender age of three, graduating to be a singer/musician/entertainer working in clubs, television and radio commercials.

A second career as a newspaper/magazine journalist and editor together with her aforementioned career gave Margot a busy working life.

The middle years of her career included running her own music school, conducting music therapy sessions for the intellectually disabled in State Government funded programs, conducting groups as a Community Educator for the State Health Department and later applying music therapy to everyday people and incorporating relationship counselling. Her highly developed intuition and positive attitude gave an added dimension of spiritual counselling.

Margot had her first autobiographical work, "Six Months to Live," published three and a half years ago in Australia.

The authors have been partners in business and life for the past 25 years.

Did you like this book?

If you enjoyed this book, you will find more interesting books at

www.CrystalDreamsPublishing.com

Please take the time to let us know how you liked this book. Even short reviews of 2-3 sentences can be helpful and may be used in our marketing materials. If you take the time to post a review for this book on Amazon.com, let us know when the review is posted and you will receive a free audiobook or ebook from our catalog. Simply email the link to the review once it is live on Amazon.com, your name, and your mailing address -- send the email to orders@mmpubs.com with the subject line "Book Review Posted on Amazon."

If you have questions about this book, our customer loyalty program, or our review rewards program, please contact us at info@mmpubs.com.

cdp
CRYSTAL DREAMS
publishing

a division of Multi-Media Publications Inc.

Speed Bumps on the Road to Enlightenment

By Dr. Janice Beaty and Julie Adams

Are you ready for a trip on the Road to Enlightenment?

This book is a wake-up call for you to become aware of what is happening behind the scenes of life. Earth is in a transitional period and her inhabitants need to prepare for a major shift in consciousness. Will it be smooth or bumpy? That's up to you.

So, wake up and take charge of your life! Be prepared to overcome the speed bumps of fear, guilt, anger, and grief with help from the Light of Love. Then fasten your seatbelts for the ride of a lifetime -- your lifetime! Are you ready?

ISBN-10:   1591460662
ISBN-13:   9781591460664
Price: $19.95

Available from Amazon.com or your nearest book retailer.
Or, order direct at www.CrystalDreamsPublishing.com.

One: Memoir of a Manic Addict

By Jennifer Marks

A wild ride through the funhouse mirror revealing the blissful horror of drugs, the odd beauty of insanity, a huge sad impossible love, the brutal truth of growing up, of pain and loss and finding the strength to make sense of the senseless and the faith to go on with the burden of living.

This true story reflects upon the party life and the hip New York City drug scene, the distorted views and insane directions launched by an undiagnosed bipolar condition kept afloat with drugs, alcohol, food binges, sex, overspending, and an inability to touch land. The author grabs hold of her own life and comes to terms with who she really is when all the craziness is stripped away: she is every woman, a vulnerable human who got lost in darkness along the way and, by the grace of God, stumbled back into the light.

ISBN-10:   15914608675
ISBN-13:   9781591460862
Price: $12.95

Available from Amazon.com or your nearest book retailer.
Or, order direct at www.CrystalDreamsPublishing.com.

Sailing on an Ocean of Tears

By Donna Kendall

Take a glimpse at the intimate and often heart-wrenching circum-stances of three women's lives as they become intertwined. Ruth is born to an impoverished, alcoholic and abusive family. She struggles to overcome her lot in life, only to discover that even well-intended decisions can lead us down the wrong path. She encounters Isabella, a vibrant Italian woman, whose deep compassion for others in need leads her away from her own chances for happiness. Bridget's hopes for happiness set her life on a course away from her native Ireland and the love of a childhood friend and into the arms of a brutal husband, intent on destroying her.

Each of their lives takes an integral path that leads them to a critical intersection where love, fate, and friendship help them to realize their greatest moment of truth.

ISBN-10:   1591460875
ISBN-13:   9781591460879
Price: $14.95

Available from Amazon.com or your nearest book retailer.
Or, order direct at www.CrystalDreamsPublishing.com

The Nurse and The Deputy

By Rod Summitt

When nurse Diane Rodgers moved to the Tri-County Area of Eastern Colorado, she was not looking for a new romance. She was only looking to escape the heartache of her broken relationship with Dr. William Stevenson. Although she had lived her whole life in Chicago, she quickly adapted to the small town life.

Deputy Sheriff Shawn White met Diane in his official capacity on her first day in the area, but quickly decided he wanted to know her personally, not professionally. His early attempts to cultivate a relationship were carefully parried by Diane, but soon his persistence appeared to be paying off. However, a misunderstanding drove a wedge between them.

When Diane finds herself in a crisis and in need of help from Shawn in his official capacity, they find that they must also confront their personal relationship head on.

ISBN-10:   1591460840
ISBN-13:   9781591460846
Price: $12.95

Available from Amazon.com or your nearest book retailer.
Or, order direct at www.CrystalDreamsPublishing.com.

Printed in the United States
131970LV00004B/4/P